Plato's *Parmenides*

PLATO'S
PARMENIDES

Constance C. Meinwald

New York   Oxford
Oxford University Press
1991

Oxford University Press

Oxford   New York   Toronto
Delhi   Bombay   Calcutta   Madras   Karachi
Petaling Jaya   Singapore   Hong Kong   Tokyo
Nairobi   Dar es Salaam   Cape Town
Melbourne   Auckland

and associated companies in
Berlin   Ibadan

Copyright © 1991 by Constance C. Meinwald

Published by Oxford University Press
200 Madison Avenue, New York, NY 10016

Oxford is a registered trademark of Oxford University Press

Library of Congress Cataloging-in-Publication Data
Meinwald, Constance C.
Plato's Parmenides / Constance C. Meinwald.
p.   cm.   Includes bibliographical references.
Includes index.
ISBN 0-19-506445-3
1. Plato. Parmenides.   2. Reasoning.   3. Socrates.
4. Zeno, of Elea.   I. Title.
B378.M45   1991   90-35419
184—dc20

1 3 5 7 9 8 6 4 2
Printed in the United States of America
on acid-free paper

ACKNOWLEDGMENTS

My work on Plato's *Parmenides* began as a 1987 doctoral dissertation at Princeton University. The present book was completed after I had joined the faculty of the University of Illinois at Chicago. Thus, I have received help on this project from many individuals. First of all, I owe thanks to Michael Frede for helping me choose my topic and for his insightful advice over the years. But others at Princeton have given vital help, especially David Furley, Sally Haslanger, Mark Johnston, and Wolfgang Mann. I am also grateful to my colleagues in the Chicago area; Elizabeth Asmis, Anil Gupta, Richard Kraut, Ian Mueller, and Nicholas White all read work in progress and discussed it with me. I am very happy to be able to thank the anonymous reader for Oxford University Press, whose sympathetic understanding of my manuscript and many useful comments were deeply appreciated.

I must acknowledge my debts to two institutions. I owe thanks to Princeton for generous support during my years as a graduate student, and for having me back as a Visiting Fellow in the spring of 1988. Another important debt is less tangible: the faculty of the Program in Classical Philosophy and its visitors have been my models in approaching ancient texts. I must also acknowledge the support of the University of Illinois at Chicago. This book took its present form during the spring of 1988, thanks to a grant from the Campus Research Board; the Philosophy Department relieved me of teaching responsibilities during the spring quarter of 1989 as well. I am deeply grateful to the members of the department for the importance they attach to nurturing the research of the junior faculty.

Chicago   C.C.M.
January 1990

CONTENTS

CONTENTS

Plato's *Parmenides*

1

Introduction

Plato's *Parmenides* today finds itself in a strange position: it is clearly an important work, but its import remains remarkably unclear. The difficulty of analyzing this text is due, in part, to its complicated structure. Within three frames we find the dialogue proper, itself consisting of two parts connected by a brief transitional section. The first part of the main dialogue is a series of rather brief exchanges enlivened by humor and some dramatic incident; the second part consists of almost thirty Stephanus pages of obscure and unadorned argument.[1] These two parts are so strikingly different that there can be no question of their being coordinate episodes of the same kind. Yet when deciding what, exactly, the character of each part is and how they fit together to make up a whole, scholars still express doubt.[2]

There is considerable interest in resolving this doubt. For one thing, certain external considerations hint at the importance of the *Parmenides*. These include the evidence of other dialogues by Plato: Socrates refers with deep respect, in both the *Theaetetus* and the *Sophist,* to Parmenides' performance on what must be the occasion depicted in our dialogue.[3] Also, the sheer compositional effort required to produce this text must have been enormous, and we would not expect Plato to expend such effort on a minor work. These hints are confirmed and given meaning in the first part of the *Parmenides*. This celebrated section presents a series of difficulties confronting Socrates as he tries to uphold views we had come to think of as constituting Plato's own theory of forms (as expressed in the *Republic* and the *Phaedo*).

Clearly, the *Parmenides* represents a crucial moment in Plato's thought. What was Plato's own attitude at this time? Did he know how to respond to the difficulties raised in the first part of the dialogue and, if so, what course did he propose? The natural starting point in answering these questions is to study the dialogue itself, to see whether the rest of the text addresses the problems. Indeed, Plato has indicated that this approach is correct: he makes Parmenides tell Socrates that the reason he has gotten into trouble is that he has posited his forms too early, before having "exercised"; the second part of the dialogue then consists of a demonstration of the kind of exercise Parmenides recommends. Since Plato meant the second part of the dialogue to bear on the problems of the first, we must understand the new exercise it contains if we wish to assess Plato's response to those problems.

But understanding the second part of the dialogue has been the single most intractable task in interpreting the *Parmenides*, if not in Plato scholarship as a whole. We are faced with an unbroken series of arguments—many seemingly so bad as to be embarrassing—systematically arranged to produce apparently contradictory conclusions. Interpreters are so divided about what this exercise achieves that disagreement still persists over whether it has any positive results at all. In my own interpretation of the exercise, which constitutes the heart of this study, I approach the arguments systematically and read them in the light of Parmenides' methodological remarks. What results is a positive and crucial innovation—a distinction between two kinds of predication—whose application enables us to recognize that the exercise consists of good arguments whose conclusions are not contradictory after all.

Since the point of the exercise is, in large part, to enable us to deal with the problems of the first part of the dialogue, I have placed my analysis of the second part of the *Parmenides* in its natural context: I precede it with a preliminary discussion of the famous problems, and I return, once I have the results of the second part of the dialogue in hand, to consider how they bear on the problems. By this point, I will have accumulated a body of evidence for my characterization of Plato's position at the moment of writing the *Parmenides*. An epilogue sets the results of my study in a larger context, namely, our understanding of Plato's development.

In this chapter, I begin with a preliminary discussion of each of the two parts of the dialogue, and of some well-known ways of interpreting them. This will prepare the reader for the scheme (outlined at the end of the chapter) that underlies my particular approach.

The First Part of the Dialogue

The first part of the *Parmenides* (if we break off before the description of the new exercise, perhaps in 135d3, just after Parmenides has congratulated Socrates on his efforts) has the appearance of a work complete in itself; in particular it resembles the canonical "Socratic" dialogue. The general pattern of these dialogues is familiar. Some philosophically interesting subject comes up in conversation. One of the persons present either holds himself out as an expert on this subject, or for some other reason can be expected to be one. This person enters into conversation with Socrates about the subject matter of his supposed expertise, answering a series of questions. By dialogue's end, the interlocutor has revealed that he is not in a position to uphold his views: his confusion is such that he has not managed to avoid contradicting himself.

The twist in our dialogue is that Socrates (here a youth) is the interlocutor, while the venerable Parmenides is the questioner. Socrates holds himself out as an expert on forms by his aggressive criticism of Parmenides' Eleatic comrade Zeno. For Socrates' criticisms are made from the standpoint of a view relying crucially on assertions about forms, and these forms are special theoretical entities. Someone who makes controversial assertions about special theoretical entities the basis for his attacks on others ought to be an expert on the relevant theory, so Socrates ought to understand forms. But, notoriously, when Parmenides questions him further about his views on forms, Socrates falls repeatedly into difficulties and admits his perplexity.

The resemblance of this fragment of the *Parmenides* to an early dialogue taken in its entirety gives it the air of something one might study by itself. Certainly the obscurity of the rest of the dialogue adds to the attraction of concentrating one's attention on this, more amenable portion of the text. In fact, a great deal of very careful work has been done to analyze particular arguments from this passage. Many of these interpretations share certain presuppositions, and I think that consideration of these assumptions will help to organize our preliminary discussion of the passage in question. For this purpose I hope it will not be too unfair to start by identifying what I take the characteristic pattern of these interpretations to be. That pattern combines concentration on the first part of the dialogue with the beliefs that each argument in the passage should be treated as a *reductio ad absurdum,* and that study of these arguments will allow us to determine whether Plato knew what to reject (and, if he did know, what it was).[4]

Despite the attractions of this approach, the dialogue contains indications that tell against it strongly.[5] First of all, this approach ignores the explicit indication of the transitional passage (135c8–137c3) that the exercise forming the second part of the dialogue is relevant to handling the problems of the first part.[6] Parmenides there tells Socrates that he will not succeed until he has done a certain exercise, which he then demonstrates in the second part of the dialogue. The implications of this connection between the two parts of the dialogue can be considered in terms of our approach to the passage or our understanding of Plato's development. In terms of our approach to the passage, the connection indicates that we should not, after all, treat the first part of the dialogue in isolation; despite its resemblance to an early dialogue it cannot be regarded as self-contained. In terms of Plato's development, the connection between the two parts of the dialogue means that we should not derive our account of Plato's development from analysis of the first part's problems only; because the dialectical exercise, according to Plato, is relevant to handling those problems, it is only fair to try to understand that exercise.

Of course, Plato might have provided an exercise to help with the problems in some merely preparatory way. We are all familiar with this type of exercise. The Galamian method for learning the violin, for example, consists solely in producing sounds that occur in no piece of music; many string players advise their students to undertake deep breathing or yoga exercises. Yet even preparatory exercises of this type are prescribed only by those who believe that in some specific way they promote the ultimate goal—by developing some prerequisite ability perhaps, or removing common impediments. Thus, the second part of the dialogue should in any case contain *some* information about Plato's attitude to the problems of the first part.[7] If it is in fact more than a merely preparatory exercise and actually does yield a response to the problems, surely that is the response to be attributed to Plato.

The second consideration involves what one might call the logical import of the passage. We have already noted that here, as in many a "Socratic *elenchos,*" we have a person who tries repeatedly to sustain conversation on some favorite subject matter, but ends each time in admitting that he has contradicted himself. This result shows, at a minimum, that the person does not have knowledge of the subject in question, for if he did (given Plato's strong conception of knowledge), he would be able to avoid contradiction. Yet the interlocutor's admission that he contradicts himself does not necessarily tell us what the *source* of the problem is. For, as we would put it, any one of the premises the interlocutor has been willing to accept may have been false, or he may, starting from true premises, have made some illicit inference from them. (I say "as we would put it" because only a formal system of logic identifies rules of inference, and thus makes it possible to categorize a particular mistake as due to a false premise or rather to an illicit inference.)

Of course, scholars differ in their views of the Socratic *elenchos:* whether, *when repeated over time,* that procedure might not have positive results; and what the status of those results would be.[8] Luckily, the difficult issue of so-called elenctic confirmation is irrelevant for our purposes, because of a difference between our exchange and those that made up Socrates' program of moral inquiry: the latter consisted of a large number of conversations with various interlocutors taking place over a long period, whereas the present exchange is clearly a unique occasion and meant to have its effect as such.

Let us return, then, to consider the case in which someone fails the *elenchos* on a single occasion. As we have noted, the fact that the interlocutor contradicts himself does not automatically prove, of any specific premise, that *it* is false. However, sometimes we are faced with an argument that has this purpose, and so it is worthwhile to consider explicitly what facts can be used in deciding when to take an argument as a *reductio ad absurdum.* It seems that the paradigmatic *reductio* works as follows: it makes explicit all of its premises, so that we can see that all but one are already known to be true, while that one is marked out as vulnerable. It then proceeds by explicit and irreproachable reasoning to derive an unacceptable conclusion. This clearly indicates that we should reject the targeted premise. Of course, many actual examples of *reductio* arguments may neglect to make all their premises and all the reasoning from them explicit; nevertheless, their basic strategy requires that they permit identification of the premise to be rejected and allow sufficient identification of the other premises involved so that the target premise can be distinguished as the most vulnerable element.

If we now approach our passage with this description of the effec-

tive *reductio* in hand, we can see how far the passage is from matching the description. (I intend to confirm the claims I make in this
paragraph in my subsequent discussion of the individual arguments.)
For one thing, the very premises that *reductio*-oriented readers wish to
reject are often unexpressed. A premise that does not appear in the
text can *a fortiori* not be marked as the target of the exercise. More
important (since we could perhaps manage to evaluate the relative vul-
nerability of the members of a group of premises if we had them), the
arguments themselves are underspecified in a strong sense. Not only
does the text often not set out enough premises for the announced
conclusion to follow, but also it is far from obvious exactly what should
be understood as completing the arguments. And different ways of
completing the arguments are not just trivially different. (The variety
of formulations of the so-called Third Man Argument produced by
careful and intelligent interpreters is a sign of the extent to which that
argument is underspecified, while the passion with which these interpreters disagree with each other indicates that the different formulations differ importantly.)

   In short, all too often in our passage the text does not effectively
target a determinate premise for destruction nor does it give us a sufficient sense of what else is involved to show that some putative target
premise is indeed the most vulnerable element—both requirements for
an author providing a *reductio*. Because Plato is so far from having
produced arguments here that follow the *reductio* strategy effectively,
we must doubt whether he can have intended the passage to function
in that way.

   Finally, we may observe that the exchanges making up the passage,
dealing with a range of issues, do not have any explicitly expressed
element in common or, more precisely, have no such substantive and
vulnerable element in common. I use the word "element" here since
it leaves open whether we are talking about some false claim with
which Socrates starts, or about some improper move he makes from
his initial claims. "Improper move" here should be understood to apply to cases we would be inclined to see as involving the addition of
a mistaken premise, as resulting from the application of a mistaken
rule of inference, or as due to a mistake in semantics (since such a
mistake can result in misinterpreting one's own claims, it too can lead
to drawing an illicit inference). The complications and potential anach-

ronism involved in distinguishing these cases combine to make the more general label useful here.

From these two observations—that Socrates has problems in a variety of areas and that no explicit and vulnerable element is common to all the arguments—we can conclude neither that one mistake underlies all his difficulties nor that each difficulty arises independently. The arguments are not presented so that they highlight any common element; still, because of the extreme underspecification of the arguments, we cannot exclude the possibility that something unexpressed is common to all or some of them. Since our plan is to return to this passage after having studied the second half of the dialogue, we will have an opportunity later to reconsider this issue. Applying what we will have learned from Parmenides' display will permit us to determine the extent to which a common treatment of these problems is available.

We can now summarize our preliminary observations on Socrates' falling into difficulties. (1) Our final response to the issues raised here is to be determined by our understanding of the second part of the dialogue. (2) The arguments that appear in this passage are extremely underspecified. (3) The exchanges show that Socrates has problems in various areas within the theory of forms he would like to advance. But these exchanges are presented in such a way as to make obvious neither the impossibility of a common treatment of the problems nor the availability of one.

It seems to me that (1) indicates that the purpose of the first part of the dialogue is introductory: it motivates us to work at the difficult developments of the second part of the dialogue, given that we have some interest in the concerns of the first part. (One might compare Book I of the *Republic,* which clearly has a purpose of this kind.) Given this purpose, (2) no longer appears to be a weakness in composition—rendering the arguments strangely ineffective in their task of proving certain claims to be false. It rather serves to help in the characterization of Socrates. His getting into trouble on the basis of sketchy arguments indicates something important about his personal level of expertise: that he is rather inexpert. This is of course compatible with the harsh evaluation that he holds determinate beliefs that are provably false. But it is equally compatible with the milder evaluation, that he is not yet able to bring to bear the specifications that would allow him to avoid trouble. According to this milder evaluation, his notions simply require further explication and understanding. Sadly, (3) indicates that a great deal of work needs to be done. But all this still leaves open the possibility that Socrates' basic motivations can be realized in an unproblematic way. Since Plato has refrained from writing the sort of passage that would force on us the harsh evaluation of Socrates, there is some hope that the milder one is what he intended. And this hope is nourished somewhat by the remarks Parmenides makes at 133b4–c1, 135a7–b2, 135b5–c3, 135c8–d3, and 135d8–e4. In these remarks, Parmenides commends Socrates for his interest in forms and his eager impulse toward arguments, says that an able person could deal even with the "greatest difficulty" that arises for form theory, and announces that forms are necessary if one is not to destroy thought and the power of *dialegesthai*. That is, even Parmenides, the poser of the problems, endorses Socrates' program.

What this passage shows about Socrates is therefore that he is not yet an adequate exponent of the theory of forms. Because of the unmistakable resemblance of Socrates' views here to those expressed by the Socrates of the middle dialogues, this passage has traditionally been regarded as a comment by Plato on the status of the so-called middle theory, but considerable disagreement has centered on the content of Plato's comment. I believe that, through this portrait of Socrates, Plato is telling us that his middle-period works did not contain a fully and adequately developed theory of forms.

Thus, as I see it, his care in being guided by Plato's text has led Gregory Vlastos rightly to coin his famous phrase that our passage is a "record of honest perplexity." [9] But whereas Vlastos's concentration on the first part of the dialogue led him to attribute the perplexity to Plato as he wrote the *Parmenides,* I believe the second part of the dialogue will show Plato himself to hold more adequate views than does the character Socrates. The immaturity of Socrates (at around twenty, he is significantly younger than he was in the preceding works) indicates that the Platonism he offers is itself somewhat immature.

I believe, then, that the overall purpose of this passage is to build up interest in the hard work that lies ahead by showing that Plato's famous middle-period presentation of forms was insufficiently developed. [10] To find out whether further development will involve rejection of any of the basic tenets, or will simply require handling them in a more sophisticated way, we must come to understand the second part of the dialogue. However, we cannot yet go on. Just as studying these problems in isolation, by ignoring their relation to the second part of the dialogue, frustrates the introductory purpose of our passage, an attempt to read the second part of the dialogue uninformed by the contents of the first part would likewise disregard the structural relation between the two parts. Preparation for the further developments of the dialogue requires that we identify the crucial notions advanced in the introductory exchange.

Given the care with which so many interpreters have studied this passage, my identification of these notions will not offer a radically new departure. What difference there is will come in my treatment of the notions. I will not be trying to make Socrates' beliefs fully determinate so as to find the false ones. Rather, in thinking about the rather vague and indefinite indications in the text, I will try to see why he agrees to certain things, and will also identify the moments at which his lack of clarity leads him into trouble.

Perhaps it will be convenient (if somewhat artificial) to start with a listing of Socrates' problem areas. The following are generally recognized:

1. He admits so readily his uncertainty about which forms there are that no argument is needed to demonstrate his lack of understanding on this point. (This is the issue some call "the extent of forms.")

2. He does not have a definite, viable understanding of what participation is. He rather has several notions on the relations of forms to sensible things, each of which appears as part of a cluster of views with which he runs into trouble. At 131a4 ff. he seems to be going on the Anaxagorean supposition that participation is having a physical share.[11] He later introduces the rather different view that participation is resemblance.

3. He makes several incompatible suggestions about the sort of things forms are (these views and his views on participation are of course not independent of each other). He sometimes treats forms as ingredients, but he also suggests that they may be thoughts, or paradigms. Again, each of these suggestions appears as part of a cluster he is unable to maintain.

4. He is willing to talk about whether participants have a share of the whole or part of the form. But without adequate notions of what

participation is, and of what sort of things forms are, this question is premature. He falls into a grossly physical interpretation of whole and part.

5. He cannot preserve the unity of his forms. This manifests itself repeatedly. Trouble looms in the whole/part arguments, whether Socrates chooses to say that each participant gets the whole of a form in which it participates or says instead that each participant gets a proper part of the form. The results of both views are supposed to threaten the form's unity: on one option the form is said to be separated from itself; on the other, it is said to be divisible. The Third Man Argument and the Likeness Regress each provides a regress in which what was originally supposed to be *the* form in question yields to an unending series of further forms. In no case is Socrates able to explain why his views do not lead to the result presented as damaging (that the forms are in two places at the same time, or divisible, or occur in unending series) or to claim that these results are not damaging after all.

6. He is not able to handle sentences of the type represented by

The Large is large,

although they play a crucial role in his explanatory scheme. Of course some readers feel that the sentence is simply false and Socrates makes a mistake in accepting it. I will instead be trying to show that in fact (and according to Plato as well) the situation is more complicated than that. At this point Socrates glimpses (rightly) that the "self-predication" sentence must express an important truth, but in his immaturity he *misinterprets* the sentence and so gets into trouble. Thus, someone who can "handle" these sentences will have a clear understanding of exactly why the sentence (in a certain use) is true.

7. He does not have enough control of his belief in the special status of forms to prevent that belief's committing him ultimately to the irrelevance of his forms to the world around us.

In part to confirm the appropriateness of this list, I shall now examine the passage, discussing each of the exchanges in turn. This discussion will also confirm the statements I made earlier about the indeterminacy of Socrates' views. But, most important, thinking about how each problem works is necessary if we are to get a feeling for the moments at which Socrates' unclear notions are leading him into trouble. This will put us in a position to apply the developments of the second part of the dialogue when we have obtained them.

In the first exchange between Socrates and Parmenides, no argument is needed to demonstrate Socrates' lack of understanding: he admits his perplexity when asked whether, in addition to forms of the just, the splendid, and the good, there are also forms of man, fire, and water; he rejects forms of hair, mud, and filth, but Parmenides announces that this is a mistake.

The first actual argument then starts (at 131a4) with Parmenides asking, "Does each participant have a share of the whole of the form or of a part?" He adds to this the second question, "Or could there be another kind of participation besides these?" This second question is obviously intended to provide support for (a presupposition of) the first one. Yet the way that Parmenides simply adds it at the end of the same utterance in which he asked the first question amounts to a suggestion that this second question does not really raise any substantive issue, to which a separate exchange should be devoted; he implies that this addition is a question whose answer is so obvious that an explicit answer is not required. In any case, the thought offered by this auxiliary question is clearly that, since there is no third option, the alternative given in the main question is legitimate.

The resulting exchange shows that Socrates does not have an adequate idea of what participation amounts to, or of what sense "whole" and "part" have in application to forms. He clearly has not thought through his position on the issue Parmenides raises. At 131a7 Socrates does not even attempt to answer the main question, whether the participant has a share of the whole form or of a part; he simply gives the expected answer to the auxiliary question, agreeing that there could be no other kind of participation besides these. Clearly a more confident interlocutor would have answered the main question. Socrates' behavior here thus adds to the impression created in the exchange just preceding, in which he admitted perplexity in the matter of the "extent of forms": he is unsure of his views on fairly obvious points connected with his positing of the forms.

In the absence of a commitment on the part of Socrates, Parmenides simply takes up the first option, that participants get the whole of the form. This option is then supposed to be problematic because if the whole form is in each of many separate participants, the form would be separate from itself. Socrates tries to contest the inference by advancing the day model (a day is present in many places at the same time without being problematically separate from itself), but Parmenides replaces this with his own model of the sail. When a sail is spread over many people, each one is covered by a part of the sail, so this change in the model turns out to introduce the second option, namely, that each participant gets only a part of the form. Then the divisibility of the form is held to threaten its unity. (Feeling the threat seems to involve abandoning commonsense intuitions guided by the case of the sail. Clearly, no one would be troubled by the worry that, since the sail is divisible, it cannot be one thing. Presumably Socrates is influenced by some notion that the forms should have a stronger kind of unity than a sail can manage to have, and he supposes that this stronger unity would be threatened by the form's divisibility.)

Instead of dropping the possibility that participants get only a part of the form, Parmenides continues exploring it (131c12 ff.). He presents Socrates with problems that arise in handling the cases of The Large, The Equal, and The Small. In the case of The Large, for example, there is supposed to be something unreasonable in dividing up The Large, giving a participant one of these parts, and then claiming that the participant is large because of this part, which is *smaller than* The Large itself.

We can understand why this seems to be problematic by supposing that Socrates is here thinking of participation in an Anaxagorean way.[12] That is, he is thinking that when something acquires a property, that property is transferred to the participant by coming with the participant's share of a form *that itself has the property*. To illustrate this kind of participation, let us say a certain stone is hot, that is, this stone participates in The Hot. An Anaxagorean analysis of this holds that The Hot itself is hot (it is the totality of heat in the world). Thus, the stone's share of The Hot is also hot, and is so in a position to endow the stone with its portion of heat, making the stone hot. In the case of a hot stone, there is not even an apparent problem with saying the stone's portion is only a part of The Hot, and so is smaller than The Hot itself. This is because being hot and being small are independent of each other.

But the three cases with which Parmenides presents Socrates are problematic, because of the properties involved. Thus, to return to the case of The Large, Socrates presumably would approach the situation by remarking that The Large is large, and that other things can become large by getting a share of it. Now comes the difficult part: the general scheme requires him to say that these shares make things large by bringing their largeness with them; however, Socrates does not know how to make this claim for the shares after it has been pointed out that they are smaller than The Large itself. The fact that something is smaller (and therefore small)[13] seems to him to rule out any claim that it is responsible for bringing largeness.

Next in order, and without any special fanfare, comes a passage (131e8 ff.) that is closely related to the Third Man Argument, which Aristotle popularized as a crucial problem for Platonism.[14] In modern times, interest in Plato's own treatment of the argument has grown as a result of the attention paid to it by Gregory Vlastos.[15] This argument is stated in terms of The Large,[16] and as far as the text goes it relies on the following considerations:

> Large things must have some one thing in common (sc. The Large).

> The Large and the other large things now require something new in common by which all of them will appear large.

This gives rise not just to a "Third Large" but is supposed to be reiterated in a way that will yield an unending series of forms. However, what we have in the text is not enough either to guarantee that this conclusion follows or to specify fully what else should be added to the argument in order to achieve that result.

We can see that some version of the claim that The Large itself is large must play some role here. Because this claim appears to many now to be a gross error, it is important to realize that in accepting it Socrates does not just make an unmotivated slip. For, as we saw, the Anaxagorean picture that lies behind his understanding of participation makes such claims as part of the basic explanatory apparatus. Moreover, the form of words guarantees that there is some truth the sentence expresses. To see this, let us start from the well-known circumstance that expressions of the form of "The Large," "The Beautiful," "The Just" can be used in Greek to refer to two very different kinds of things. "The Just," for example, can refer on the one hand to something that happens to be just (or to whatever does), and on the other to what it is about these things that is just. Similarly, "The

Beautiful'' could be used of vases, or of Helen, but could also be used
to refer to what is beautiful about these things. Abstract nouns like
"Justice" and "Beauty" come to be used increasingly in Plato's time
as a way of being unambiguous in one's reference to the second kind
of thing; Plato himself uses both forms of words.

For our present purposes, we [17] should reflect on the fact that in
describing the second kind of use we employ phrases like "what is
just about just things," "what it is about Helen that is beautiful." In
these phrases "just" and "beautiful" are *already being predicated*.
This guarantees that

The Just is just (or Justice is Just)

and

The Beautiful is beautiful (or Beauty is beautiful)

must hold. They do no more than repeat the predications we accepted
within the relative clauses glossing our subject terms. To interpret these
sentences may be difficult, but without making up one's mind about
how they are to be understood, one can see they express some truths.
(It is the fact that a competent speaker can just *see* that sentences so
framed must express truths that accounts for Protagoras's acceptance
of "Justice is just" [*Protagoras* 330c3–7]. He precisely does not have
a Platonist metaphysics and so could not be accepting the sentence as
an expression of some extravagant philosophical view.)

To find out the appropriate interpretation of these sentences and so
to identify which truths they express require not only progress in semantics but some foundational work in metaphysics. (This is work, as
we will see in the course of our study, that Plato has undertaken.) But
now we can already see that the importance of claims of the form in
question to Socrates' explanatory apparatus and the guarantee that sentences of that form do express some truth together make it inappropriate to reject "The Large is large" as simply false. Rather, Plato
ideally should recognize that on one interpretation (the one we post-
Aristotelian readers most naturally give it) it is trivially false, but also
find another interpretation for it, on which it will be true.

As I explained earlier, I will be deriving my account of Plato's
response to the Third Man (and to the other problems of the first part
of the dialogue) from my study of the second part of the dialogue; I
regard as mistaken any attempt to derive a response (Plato's or one's

own "diagnostic" one) to this problem from one's formulation of the argument, and as no less mistaken the production for this purpose of a determinate formulation. For the present then, let us simply note that whatever reasons Socrates may have for accepting the argument Parmenides offers, he does accept it, sees it as problematic, and in so doing shows once more that he is not in a position competently to deal with the entities he is so eager to introduce.

Socrates tries unsuccessfully to get around the Third Man problem by offering in turn the suggestions that forms are thoughts, and that they are paradigms. The suggestion that forms are paradigms brings with it the notion that participation is resemblance, and when this turns out to lead to difficulty (the Likeness Regress), we find explicit mention of the need to find out what participation is (133a5–6).

The fact that Socrates makes these suggestions about forms and participation adds to our picture of him as lacking a definite and viable view of his own most crucial notions. However, we should also note that these suggestions do not have the same status as the Third Man Argument itself. Since they are made as a way around it, there would be no need for them if Socrates became able to handle the Third Man *in some other way.*

Although the Third Man is usually thought to be *the* argument against Socrates, Plato clearly did not see it as the only serious difficulty, since he made Parmenides refer to another one as the "greatest" and placed this greatest difficulty prominently, at the end of the series, at 133b4 ff. (Perhaps a comment on the sense in which this difficulty can be the greatest is also in order here. It certainly does not strike many now as harder to deal with than the Third Man. Plato may mean not that this problem is the hardest to handle, but rather that this difficulty, if not handled, involves the worst result.[18] For the difficulty, although it initially seems to be concerned only with forms associated with relations [as Mastership is associated with the mastery relation], ultimately leads to the consequence that no forms can do their basic job of explaining the sensible world and grounding our knowledge of it.)

The difficulty takes its starting point from the conjunction of the claim that since forms are *kath' heauta* they cannot be in us *(en hēmin),* with the observation that forms associated with relations have their being *(ousia)* in relation to other forms and not in relation to the things around us, whereas the things around us are related to other things around us and not to the forms. To take an example perhaps more congenial to our sensibilities than the ones that appear in the text, we are the siblings of each other, not of the forms; nor do the forms have us as their relatives, for they are relatives only to each other.

To see how the difficulty develops, we can follow the sample argument given in the text in terms of Knowledge and its special branches (not identified more particularly), and see how the argument would go in the particular case of Arithmetic. In the case of Arithmetic, the claim about the patterns of relations yields:

> Arithmetic knows The Numbers (and presumably not anything around us).

> The knowledge of this world *(par' hēmin)* knows numerous collections of objects around us (and presumably not The Numbers).

Now since the knowledge of this world (which we might have) does not know The Numbers, and since we are obviously not Arithmetic Itself, nor do we have it among or in us (by the claim that the status of forms prevents their being *en hēmin* = in us),

> We do not know The Numbers.

A fortiori we are not in a position to apply knowledge of The Numbers in order to derive our knowledge of numerous collections of objects around us. Moreover, there is no such application of Arithmetic to the sensible world. For, by the claim about the patterns of relations, only *we and the things around us,* and not Arithmetic, are related to sensible objects. Given the explicitly made point that the particular branches of knowledge know the particular forms, we can see that the availability of this type of argument will prevent us from knowing any of the forms and will also prevent any knowledge of the forms from explaining our world at all.[19]

The stress in setting up this problem on the claim that the forms in question have their *ousia* only in relation to *(pros)* forms, whereas we are what we are only in relation to other sensible particulars indicates that it will bear on this problem if we come to see that there *is* a way in which sensible particulars have their being in relation to forms. Socrates now thinks he cannot posit such a relation without thereby making forms degenerate into just more mundane things around us.

In general, these arguments show that Socrates is unable to handle adequately notions that may yet be successfully developed. (I do not mean that, for example, the suggestion that participation is resemblance must survive, but that at least *some* notion of participation will.) I will return, in chapter 9, to consider how Plato can be seen, in light of the developments of the second part of the dialogue, to have outgrown the problems of the present passage. Now, realizing that this application is promised if we work at the dialectical exercise, let us turn to preliminary characterization of the second part of the *Parmenides*.

The Second Part of the Dialogue

We come now to the dialectical exercise (also called "gymnastic dialectic" for the sake of variety, since *gymnasia* means exercise). It is perhaps as well to start by mentioning what is plainly the most striking feature of this strange production: it consists wholly in sections of argument arranged in such a way that the conclusions of the first section seem to be in systematic contradiction with those of the second, and so on. Thus the dialogue ends with Parmenides summarizing his results in the remarkable formulation:

Εἰρήσθω τοίνυν τοῦτό τε καὶ ὅτι, ὡς ἔοικεν, ἓν εἴτ᾽ ἔστιν εἴτε μὴ ἔστιν, αὐτό τε καὶ τἆλλα καὶ πρὸς αὑτὰ καὶ πρὸς ἄλληλα πάντα πάντως ἐστί τε καὶ οὐκ ἔστι καὶ φαίνεταί τε καὶ οὐ φαίνεται. (166c2–5)

Let this be said therefore, and that, as it appears, if The One is or is not, it and the others in relation to themselves and in relation to each other are all things in all ways and are not, and seem and seem not.

Aristotle (the interlocutor) replies:

Ἀληθέστατα. (166c5)

Most true.

The sheer magnitude of the exercise—it must be the longest unbroken stretch of argument in the entire Platonic corpus—suggests that it achieves substantial results. Yet no interpretation of this text has identified those results conclusively.

One might seek for help from the extremely labored description Parmenides gives of the exercise in the preceding transitional section. Unfortunately, that description is itself somewhat opaque: Parmenides urges Socrates to repeat the exercise, taking each of the forms in turn as a subject, and deriving certain specified sets of results in each case (135d8–136c5). But the force of one crucial pair of specifications that Parmenides employs throughout his description is unexplained, and this makes it impossible adequately to understand his advice. Socrates in fact says immediately that he has not understood the advice, and asks Parmenides to demonstrate the exercise he recommends (136c7–8). (Parmenides' response to this request will be the second part of the dialogue.) Since Socrates has been presented as able and promising, if immature, this touch suggests that Plato was aware that Parmenides' methodological remarks are not fully intelligible on their own. He has in effect drawn our attention to the need to be guided by Parmenides' dialectical display in order fully to understand his methodological remarks.

Since neither the methodological advice nor the dialectical display is fully intelligible on its own, we must ultimately resort to using the methodological advice to help us interpret the actual exercise, and vice versa. We can note now, however, that, having agreed to display the exercise, Parmenides says he will start from his own hypothesis about The One. So (in accordance with the description) he produces sections of argument starting from each member of the pair:

If The One is

and

If The One is not.

Since the most striking feature of these arguments is their resulting systematically in apparent contradictions, it is convenient to consider different possible interpretations by identifying different responses to this formal feature. I would like to discuss two main types of response.[20] (I ignore the possibility, if it is one, of embracing contradiction.)

The first basic kind of interpretation takes as its starting point an understanding of the contradictions as real. This produces a need to find things to reject. The second type of interpretation supposes the contradictions to be only apparent. Since the results of the dialectical exercise are not contradictory on this view, this type of interpretation has the potential to show that we can follow the lead of the interlocutor and accept all the conclusions.

Let us consider each of these approaches in turn. The first, taking the contradictions to be real, is committed to the unacceptability of the overall result of the dialectic. Thus, unless Plato is to be seen as producing a monumental record of confusion, this type of interpretation must suppose that Plato's purpose is to display certain mistakes in order to motivate us to recognize and reject them. That is, this type of interpretation leads naturally to "rejectionism." One could characterize particular kinds of rejectionism by distinguishing specific choices of what is to be rejected. But for present purposes it is sufficient to consider rejectionism generally.

The rejectionist stance does receive support from the circumstance that some of the individual arguments have always looked rather embarrassingly bad. But it also has five disadvantages. The first becomes apparent if we compare the response of our interlocutor, Aristotle, with that typical of the interlocutors in the Socratic dialogues. In those works we commonly find that at least one contradiction appears to obtain among the things to which the interlocutor has committed himself; Plato has made us familiar with a common response to this. For in the Socratic dialogues, when this point is reached, the interlocutor and Socrates *remark* on the fact, drawing attention to the appearance of the contradiction as problematic to the point of being unacceptable. Often the discussion extends into professions of confusion or dissatisfaction with the situation, and sometimes into an entertaining diagnosis of Socrates as a source of trouble or a pronouncement that the matter at hand has not been understood. Through such passages these dialogues provide us with (the beginnings of) an interpretative response to the result of the dialectic. For whether or not we accept the diagnosis offered, we find ourselves in agreement with the participants in recognizing that something has gone wrong.

The situation regarding Parmenides' gymnastic dialectic is completely different. For although the incidence of grammatical contradictions is much higher and more systematic than in the Socratic dialogues, and many of the individual conclusions are as superficially paradoxical as they could be, there are no expressions of dissatisfaction at these results.[21] The absence of such mention is at its most notable at the end of the dialogue, where Parmenides summarizes the results of the dialogue in a way (quoted previously) that clearly highlights their paradoxical character. Yet the interlocutor not only expresses no dissatisfaction at this formulation but goes to an extreme in accepting it by means of the superlative form *Alēthestata* ("Most true").

One response to this acceptance on the part of the interlocutor is to construe him as being so demoralized, intimidated, confused, or incompetent as not really to be playing an active role. However, the role of the interlocutor in all other forms of dialectic is so central as to make it unlikely that anything lacking this feature could be introduced as a kind of dialectic. Moreover, the incompetence of the interlocutor would render pointless any exercise consisting of obtaining his assent to a series of arguments; even the lesson of observing how a particular kind of character can lead someone into a particular kind of mistake is unavailable, since Aristotle is unusually undercharacterized (except for the bare facts that he has talked with Socrates, is the youngest, and later became one of the Thirty, we learn nothing about him). If we take seriously the idea that Aristotle is an adequate respondent, the fact that he accepts the dialogue's conclusions vehemently—despite their being put in a way that is deliberately and extensively paradoxical—is significant. It is an indication from within the dialogue against making rejectionism our interpretative response.

Next, the description of the paradigmatic *reductio ad absurdum* (developed earlier, in connection with the problems of the first part of the dialogue) does not match this exercise well. What is missing here, in argument after argument, is the targeting of the vulnerable element. This absence seems to be the reason for two features of interpretations of this type. One is that this rejectionist reading works better when an argument is removed from its actual context and placed instead within the history of some notable philosophical confusion—the history then does the job of highlighting the target. The other is that capable interpreters following this approach do not obtain results in agreement with each other. I believe this to be due to their being forced to fall back on their own intuitions about what must go (since the text does not indicate this). This type of interpretation thus comes too close to determining Plato's view on the basis of our own.

The third disadvantage of the rejectionist approach is that, regarding the exercise as a sampler of mistakes, it has little tendency to show the *Parmenides* to be unified. A lack of unity would not only be ironic in the case of a work about unity, but it would make the *Parmenides* an anomaly among Plato's works.

The fourth problem is that, if the rejectionist scheme is to explain away all the contradictory results, then fully half of the arguments will be required to have something wrong with them. Despite the apparent poor quality of some, the expectation that so many arguments can be rejected is unrealistic.[22] (The actual study of the particular arguments that lies ahead will confirm this claim.)

The scheme's final disadvantage is that rejectionist interpretations in practice yield results that make it hard to account for Parmenides' exhortation to repeat the exercise, taking in turn a series of subjects. For example, Owen's influential "map"[23] of the exercise gives prominence to "I/P confusion" (confusion between the identifying and predicative uses of "S is P"). Presumably anyone who benefits from the exercise as Owen understands it will have learned to beware of I/P confusions quite generally; it would be eccentric to think of the moral of the exercise as: do not confuse the identifying and predicative uses of "S *is one*." Again, the moral is general if what leads to trouble is the failure to see that a form should not be made to bear any predicates at all (what Ryle calls the "most tempting reading"),[24] or if the point is the opposite one that "there cannot be anything which is just one simple property in the sense that nothing can be predicated of it."[25] Ryle's "most tempting reading" and Curd's presentation[26] of her view both make explicit that the moral in question goes for all forms. And such a general moral does seem more substantial than results only about The One would be. But if interpretations of the exercise leave nothing of interest to be gained in connection with other potential subjects, they deprive the recommended repetitions of any point.

These five disadvantages together tell strongly against rejectionism. Since the type of interpretation that takes the contradictions between sections to be real leads naturally to rejectionism (lest it take Plato to be incompetent), we should avoid that first type of interpretation. This means turning to an interpretation of the second main type, which construes the contradictions as merely apparent. Within this group, however, are variations. As noted previously, with the overall result of the dialectic no longer understood as contradictory, this type of interpretation has the potential to show how we can accept all the arguments and their conclusions, thus avoiding rejectionism, the natural concomitant of the first type of interpretation. But although rejectionism does not follow naturally from the starting point of this interpretation, it is not wholly incompatible with it either. The recognition that the dialectic's results are not in real contradiction with each other does not exclude the possibility of believing that certain conclusions are unacceptable for other reasons. We will thus find among interpretations of the second type some "mixed" ones[27] that combine recognition that there are no real contradictions in the dialectic's results (thus qualifying as of the second type) with rejectionism (the natural concomitant of the first type).

Of course, interpretations of this second main type cannot simply assert that the contradictions are merely apparent; they must explain this further. Whereas in the abstract we can see there must be various ways of achieving this, in practice there is one primary way in which it has been done: by supposing that different sections of argument deal with different subjects. That supposition is the basis of the interpretation associated with Neoplatonism, and also of that developed in our own century by Francis Cornford. Now clearly, if The One of one section is not the same entity as The One of another, there is no threat of real contradiction in results like

The One does not move

and

The One moves

if they occur in different sections. Thus, the basic claim of the multiple-subject type of interpretation enables it to dispose satisfactorily of the threat of contradiction, putting it in a position to go on to construe all the arguments as acceptable and as meant to establish their conclusions.

These are, of course, additional steps. While Cornford, in fact, upholds the validity of the arguments and recognizes that the conclusions do not contradict each other, he finds other reasons to object to some of them. He thus turns out to reject, for example, the postulation of the subject of the first section of arguments. In effect, he produces a "mixed" interpretation that is vulnerable to both (some of) the criticisms of rejectionism already noted as well as to those to come of multiple-subject interpretations. Until now, the logical potential of this type of interpretation to accept all the conclusions of the dialectic has been fulfilled only by the Neoplatonist tradition.

Since the interpretations viewing the contradictions as merely apparent that have actually been developed have been of the multiple-subject type, let us consider now the weaknesses associated with positing different subjects for different sections of argument. The first and most important derives from the circumstance that this kind of interpretation, with its multiple Ones, gives different interpretations to the hypothesis

If The One is

in its different occurrences. This conflicts with the fact that the hypothesis itself is supposed to be always the same.[28] It could not be the same if it were not always about the same subject.

Second, multiple-subject interpreters must explain why Plato wants to discuss the subjects they distinguish. Insofar as their explanations rely on the special history of The One, they will be left with the last limitation of the rejectionist approach: their interpretation will be no better suited to explain Parmenides' demand to keep repeating the exercise with different subjects. For example, Plato's purpose as Cornford has it is to explode Eleatic Monism (understood as a doctrine about an undesirable One, which is the only thing that is) and replace it with a remodeled Pythagoreanism (positing a different One that serves as a principle of indefinitely many other things that are). This does nothing to explain what the purpose of the exercise is to be when the subject is, say, Motion, nor can it be extended in any obvious way to do so. So the multiple-subject interpreters, opposite to the rejectionists in so many ways, seem actually to attach *too much* importance to the fact that The One is the subject of Parmenides' display. For Parmenides' demand to make sense, The One will have to be something more than an arbitrary subject, but something less than uniquely suited to the exercise.

The multiple-subject interpretation, then, creates serious problems by its basic move of distinguishing various Ones. Moreover, our discussion of it allows us to rule out a further class of possible interpretations of this second main type. For we have seen that the multiple-subject interpretation runs into trouble in part because positing different subjects changes the hypotheses inappropriately. This puts us in a position to rule out *any* scheme that would (by whatever expedient) uphold the validity of the arguments by giving different interpretations to

If The One is

in its different occurrences.

However, the positing of different subjects (or, in general, different hypotheses) for different sections is clearly only one way of producing an interpretation of the second main type—that is, of construing the contradictions as merely apparent. What we need is an interpretation that will fulfill the promise of this general type to avoid rejectionism, without taking on those associated with the positing of multiple subjects. Thus we must: (a) show that the conclusions of all the arguments do follow, (b) show that the contradictions between sections are merely apparent, and (c) avoid giving different interpretations to the hypotheses themselves in their different occurrences.

This is what my interpretation undertakes to do. Guided by consideration (a) and by the methodological remarks of the transitional section, I will develop a distinction between *two kinds of predication*. One immediate result of this development is that, when faced with paired results from different sections of the form

A is B and not (A is B),

I will not interpret both occurrences of "A is B" in the same way, and thus I will fulfill condition (b). Because this new way of construing the conclusions will rely only on the kind of predication involved in them, it will not posit different subjects or multiply the hypotheses in any way, which means it will satisfy requirement (c).

This interpretation of the dialectical exercise will receive confirmation when we turn to the larger issues. For one thing, it shows how the second part of the *Parmenides* fulfills its role in relation to the first part: with the new development (and associated developments in the underlying metaphysics), Plato will have outgrown the problems of the introductory exchange. Equally important, my interpretation will give us an understanding of the dialectical exercise on which the demand for repetition makes sense. Indeed, the lesson that there are two kinds of predication, and the advantages of the lesson in avoiding the famous problems, can be derived from Parmenides' demonstration alone. But as my study will show, repetition of the exercise will bring forward substantial results in addition to those of the present inquiry; in fact, the exercise is designed to display all the results concerning the structural relations of the basic explanatory entities and also their role in the world that it is the purpose of Platonism to obtain.

General Overview

In what follows, my main task will be to develop an account of the crucial innovation that emerges from the second part of the dialogue. Chapter 2 will deal with two issues concerning the interpretation of Parmenides' methodological remarks: the structure of the exercise he recommends, and the particular hypothesis he takes as the starting point for his demonstration. In chapter 3, I will develop my interpretation of the crucial pair of specifications Parmenides uses in describing the new kind of exercise. This will lead to the distinction between two kinds of predication. Chapters 4 through 8 will be devoted to confirming that, when read with the help of this distinction, the arguments presented are good ones. At the same time, we will be observing what they tell us about The One: the various ways in which its position in the world is preeminent. Then, in chapter 9, I will return to the problems of the first part of the dialogue, offering the solutions I think Plato intended for those difficulties. Chapter 10 will place the *Parmenides* in its larger context: I will conclude my study by considering what it contributes to our understanding of Plato's development.

2

The Dialectical Scheme

The transitional section of the *Parmenides* occurs at 135c8–137c3. I call it "transitional" because of its role in connecting the exchange between Parmenides and Socrates (which revealed Socrates' inability to uphold his views about forms) with the second part of the dialogue (Parmenides' dialectical display). The transition is effected as follows: Parmenides tells Socrates that before he can get things right he will have to do a certain kind of exercise, involving the deriving of certain specified sets of results from a series of so-called hypotheses. Parmenides describes the exercise repeatedly. First he describes what the exercise would amount to when starting from Zeno's hypothesis and then in the case of the hypothesis: if Likeness is. He continues with a general description of the exercise that abstracts from the particular choice of subject (or associated hypothesis). When Socrates says that he has not understood this advice, Parmenides is prevailed upon to demonstrate the exercise. Before starting his display, he announces what hypothesis he will take.

Clearly this transitional section is of great importance. For one thing, we can expect these methodological remarks to provide guidance in understanding the second part of the dialogue: Parmenides' own description of the exercise must be of paramount importance in interpreting the arguments that constitute its demonstration. And given the well-attested difficulty of arriving at a satisfactory interpretation of those arguments, we cannot afford to ignore any available source of guidance. More broadly, since the repetition of this exercise is said by Plato to be a necessary precondition for progress in metaphysics, there is considerable interest in coming to understand what the exercise in general is supposed to achieve. Clearly paying close attention to this passage, in which it is introduced and described, is the starting point for that project. (In fact, as I mentioned in chapter 1, because of the extremely abstract character of this passage, we will not be able to develop a complete understanding of the exercise until we have joined our analysis of these methodological remarks to study of the arguments themselves.)

Three questions concerning the dialogue's transitional section will be considered in this and the following chapter. First, what is the structure of the exercise Parmenides is recommending (i.e., what number of sections of argument does he prescribe, how does he characterize those sections, and in what order are they to be produced)? Second, what is the hypothesis from which Parmenides will derive results in his demonstration of the exercise? Third, what is the force of a certain pair of specifications (which I will be calling "the in-relation-to qualifications") that Parmenides uses throughout his characterization of the recommended sections of argument?

It may seem strange that I order the questions in this way, since the second is a question about Parmenides' particular display, whereas the first and third concern the exercise taken generally. But I will be taking them up in the order listed; indeed, I will postpone my answer to the third question until the next chapter. This grouping is based on the kind of discussion that will be involved in each case. Treatment of the third question will ultimately require thinking about individual arguments from the second part of the dialogue, and will turn out to lead directly to the innovation I believe to be the main achievement of the *Parmenides*. Before proceeding to that, I will deal in the present chapter with the other questions about the transitional section. Discussion of both of them will involve consideration of the editing of the relevant passages. These passages in the editions of Burnet and Diès are extremely problematic, seeming to be incompatible with their context. Thus, the transitional section seems to be internally incoherent. Moreover, Parmenides' general description of the exercise and announcement of his hypothesis appear to be incompatible with the actual display that follows—that is, both editions have Parmenides saying he will do one thing, but then doing quite another.

All this is clearly most unsatisfactory. Nevertheless, virtually all writers on the dialogue seem to be basing their translations and paraphrases of the passages in question on these editions, without commenting on the incoherent character of the utterances they thereby attribute to Parmenides. In the case of the first of the problematic passages, I will show how matters can be remedied simply by aban-

doning the view of the structure of the exercise that is encouraged by
the punctuation recent editors have supplied. (As far as I know, the
role of the punctuation in contributing to the problem has not been
remarked. Yet since punctuation is the work of editors and not part of
Plato's text, changing punctuation is always an attractive and conservative way to resolve problems.) In the case of Parmenides' announcement of his hypothesis, Max Wundt has proposed two alternative conjectures that correct the problem by yielding the desired pair
of hypotheses "If The One is" and "If The One is not" unambiguously. I will advocate following him.[1] I have grouped these discussions together for what I hope will be the convenience of readers.
While the inquiry of this chapter is important, I recognize that some
readers may not care to follow the details of this kind of study. They
can simply proceed to chapter 3 after consulting pp. 36–37 (where the
structure of the exercise indicated by my discussion is laid out in the
section entitled "Ordering of Reading II").

Let us turn now to the transitional methodological remarks themselves.
Parmenides' description of the exercise he urges Socrates to undertake
is lengthy and labored. He first remarks that one must not only hypothesize that a thing is (or: is the case) and examine the results from
one's hypothesis, but one must also hypothesize that the same thing is
not (or: is not the case) (135e9–136a2). He then goes on to give a
series of descriptions that specify the kinds of results one is supposed
to derive. The first description tells us what the exercise would amount
to if it started from Zeno's hypothesis: *ei polla estin* ("If ⟨the things
that are⟩ are many," or "If Many is."[2] Jowett contrives to preserve
the ambiguity, translating "on the hypothesis of the being of the many";[3]
I will follow him in this.) The second gives instructions concerning
what to do if one's hypothesis is: If Likeness is. (I shall subsequently
refer to these two descriptions as "the particular descriptions of the
exercise"). They run as follows:

εἰ πολλά ἐστι, τί χρὴ συμβαίνειν καὶ αὐτοῖς τοῖς πολλοῖς πρὸς
αὐτὰ καὶ πρὸς τὸ ἕν καὶ τῷ ἑνὶ πρός τε αὐτὸ καὶ πρὸς τὰ πολλά·
καὶ αὖ εἰ μή ἐστι πολλά, πάλιν σκοπεῖν τί συμβήσεται καὶ τῷ
ἑνὶ καὶ τοῖς πολλοῖς καὶ πρὸς αὐτὰ καὶ πρὸς ἄλληλα· (136a5–b1)

⟨You should examine⟩ what must follow both for The Many themselves
in relation to themselves and in relation to The One, and for The One

in relation to itself and in relation to The Many, on the hypothesis of the being of The Many, and ⟨you should⟩ in turn examine what will follow for The One and The Many in relation to themselves and in relation to each other, on the hypothesis of the nonbeing of The Many.

καὶ αὖθις αὖ ἐὰν ὑποθῇ εἰ ἔστιν ὁμοιότης ἢ εἰ μὴ ἔστιν, τί ἐφ' ἑκατέρας τῆς ὑποθέσεως συμβήσεται καὶ αὐτοῖς τοῖς ὑποτεθεῖσιν καὶ τοῖς ἄλλοις καὶ πρὸς αὐτὰ καὶ πρὸς ἄλληλα. (136b1– b4)

And again if you hypothesize if Likeness is, or if it is not, what on each hypothesis will follow for the very things hypothesized and for the others, in relation to themselves and in relation to each other.

Parmenides then mentions a few more subjects that should be treated in the same way and concludes with a general description of the exercise that abstracts from the particular subject (or associated hypothesis) one might choose. It is this general description we want to understand. But the circumstance that the relationship of each of the preliminary descriptions to the final one clearly is that of particular to general will be useful to us: since Parmenides is always describing *the same procedure,* we have to understand the general description in a way that makes it compatible with the particular descriptions preceding it.

We now come to the question of the structure of the exercise Parmenides is recommending here. This is problematic because the general description of the exercise is written in such a way that factors such as punctuation, which are up to the discretion of interpreters, affect what it is saying. The interpretative decisions in question affect the structure of the exercise indicated to the extent of determining the number of sections of argument to be produced, their kind, and the order in which they are to be attempted.

Let us start by considering the text as presented in the editions now in print, and see what readings are possible. Burnet punctuates as follows:

καὶ ἑνὶ λόγῳ, περὶ ὅτου ἂν ἀεὶ ὑποθῇ ὡς ὄντος καὶ ὡς οὐκ ὄντος καὶ ὁτιοῦν ἄλλο πάθος πάσχοντος, δεῖ σκοπεῖν τὰ συμβαίνοντα πρὸς αὑτὸ καὶ πρὸς ἓν ἕκαστον τῶν ἄλλων, ὅτι ἂν προέλῃ, καὶ πρὸς πλείω καὶ πρὸς σύμπαντα ὡσαύτως· καὶ τἆλλα αὖ πρὸς αὑτά τε καὶ πρὸς ἄλλο ὅτι ἂν προαιρῇ ἀεί, ἐάντε ὡς ὂν ὑποθῇ ὃ

ὑπετίθεσο, ἄντε ὡς μὴ ὄν, εἰ μέλλεις τελέως γυμνασάμενος
κυρίως διόψεσθαι τὸ ἀληθές. (136b6–c5)

Diès's edition differs from Burnet's only in one particular—not of
punctuation, but of word order—which has no bearing on our concern.

This punctuation tends to suggest that the exercise in question has
two main halves, one of which is described by the text printed before
the semicolon, and the other after. Given this, there are four main
ways of reading the passage. For the sake of completeness, I will
evaluate the merits of each in turn. (In fact, the last one is not only
implausible but, as far as I know, has had no adherents. The others
are implausible in varying degrees.) At this stage, paraphrases will be
more useful than complete translations; I will postpone giving a full
translation until I have determined which reading is preferable.

Reading Ia

> In the case of whatever one has hypothesized as being or as not being
> or as suffering any other affection, one must examine the consequences
> that result from the hypothesis for the subject in relation to itself, and
> for the subject in relation to the others. Then one must derive results
> for the others in relation to themselves and for the others in relation to
> the subject (which was hypothesized to be or not to be).

Presumably no one would endorse an interpretation of the dialectic
based on taking this literally; it has two serious problems. First, the
advice so understood prescribes the deriving of consequences from a
single hypothesis only. (This reading takes the opening statement of
three possible hypotheses as options from which only one will have
been selected on any particular occasion of doing the exercise, and
recommends the use of no hypothesis additional to the one initially
selected.) This goes against the injunction at 135e9 ff. to derive results
not only from one's original hypothesis but also from its negation.[4] It
also makes the general description of the exercise fail to match the
particular descriptions (quoted earlier) that started from Zeno's hypothesis and from the hypothesis about Likeness. For both of those
descriptions obeyed the injunction—that is, they went on (unlike this
description on this reading) to prescribe sections of argument to be
derived from the negation of the original hypothesis.

Second, this reading makes this crucial description rather careless.

Whereas three forms that one's initial hypothesis might take are actually specified at the opening (as the beginning of the paraphrase has them, "In the case of whatever one has hypothesized as being or as not being or as having any other affection"), by the end only two are remembered (the end of the paraphrase refers to "the subject [which was hypothesized to be or not to be]").

Reading Ib

Everything that one hypothesizes as being, one must also hypothesize as not being, and as suffering any other affection whatever. One must derive (from each of these three antecedents) what results for the subject in relation to itself and for the subject in relation to the others. Then one must derive results for the others in relation to themselves and for the others in relation to the subject, from each of the two following antecedents: if what one hypothesized is, and again if it is not.

This reading also has several problems. The first derives from its specifying three antecedents that must be used to derive results for the subject (one must hypothesize it as being, and also as not being, *and also as suffering any other affection whatever*). We may wonder why, for example, if we want to start from the hypothesis "If Motion is," we should be required also to hypothesize "If Motion is pink." Even harder to see is why we must use this third type of antecedent when generating results for the subject *but not* when generating results for the others. But the exercise is presented as being asymmetric in this way. For when we reach its specifications of results for the others, we find only two antecedents: if what one hypothesized is, and again if it is not. This asymmetry is not only perplexing on its own, but it finds no correlate in the particular descriptions that preceded this general case: when the exercise was described as starting from Zeno's hypothesis and from the hypothesis about Likeness, there was no mention of any third antecedent such as we find here.

The second problem also involves comparison with the particular descriptions. This reading specifies that all the results for the subject are to be obtained first, and then one is to go on to derive results for the others. The particular descriptions do not group the sections in this way. Rather, they make the main division between the results from the positive hypothesis and those from the negative one. This is especially clear in the case of the description of the exercise starting from

Zeno's hypothesis (quoted previously). The division is there strengthened not just by the editors' semicolon after *pros ta polla* (in 136a7)
but by *kai au* and *palin* in the same line, which clearly mark a new
beginning from the negative hypothesis.

Reading Ic

In the case of whatever one has hypothesized as being or as not being
or as suffering any other affection, one must examine the consequences
that result from the hypothesis for the subject in relation to itself, then
for the subject in relation to the others. Then one must derive results
for the others in relation to themselves and for the others in relation to
the subject, from each of these two antecedents: if what one hypothesized is the case, and if it is not the case.

This has drawbacks similar to those of Reading Ib. It introduces an
asymmetry within Parmenides' description, for it specifies that one
must obtain results for the subject from only the original hypothesis
(which may take any of three possible forms), and then goes on to
specify results to be derived for the others from each of two antecedents. This reading also makes a major division between results for the
subject and those for the others. As we have seen, both of these features fail to correspond to the relevant parts of the particular descriptions.

Reading Id

Everything that one hypothesizes as being, one must also hypothesize
as not being, and as suffering any other affection, and derive (using
each of these three antecedents) what results for the subject in relation
to itself and for the subject in relation to the others. Then one must
derive results for the others in relation to themselves and for the others
in relation to the subject (which was hypothesized to be or not to be).

We can drop this reading immediately. It makes no sense to end by
referring to a subject "which was hypothesized to be or not to be," if
one has already presupposed (beginning of paraphrase) that the subject
has been hypothesized as being. This reading also gives the most glar-
ing asymmetry of all: it gives three antecedents to be used in deriving
results for the subject, and stipulates none to be used in deriving re-

sults for the others. (To make the plan usable, we could possibly understand that the same three antecedents that were used in deriving results for the subject are to be reused for the others.) This reading also gives the now-familiar wrong order, mentioning all the results for the subject first, and then all of those for the others.

We have explored four possible ways of understanding the text, following the standard punctuation and the main division of the exercise it suggests. The reason there are four is that at 136b7–8 the occurrences of *kai* may be equivalent to *ē* (i.e., "and" here may be equivalent to "or"; cf. *pour les peaux sèches et sensibles*). On the other hand, they may not be. And similarly with the occurrences of *-te* in 136c4. Having examined all four combinations of the "and's" and "or's", we have still not found a satisfactory reading of this important general description of the dialectical exercise. To seek a different kind of reading, we must first abandon the break Burnet and Diès suggest after *hōsautōs* at 136c2. This finally makes possible the reading I prefer:[5]

Reading II

One's initial hypothesis may have any one of the following three forms: something is, something is not, or something has any other affection. One starts from this hypothesis, and must derive results from it for the subject in relation to itself, and for the subject in relation to the others, and then for the others in relation to themselves and for the others in relation to the subject. One next goes on to suppose that what one originally hypothesized is not the case, and derives in turn results for the subject in relation to itself, and for the subject in relation to the others, and then for the others in relation to themselves and finally for the others in relation to the subject.

On this reading,

περὶ ὅτου ἂν ἀεὶ ὑποθῇ ὡς ὄντος καὶ ὡς οὐκ ὄντος καὶ ὁτιοῦν ἄλλο πάθος πάσχοντος

specifies three forms one's initial hypothesis may take (something is, something is not, or something has any other affection).[6] We now do not make the passage's main articulation after *hōsautōs* (one could help to show this by changing the semicolon the editors have placed there back to the comma of the Aldine edition). Thus, it is no longer the case that (roughly) the first half of the passage describes results for the subject, while the second half is devoted entirely to describing results for the others. For it is now possible to take *eante hōs on . . . ante hōs mē on* in 136c4 as going with everything that has preceded it, instead of being confined to the second half of the passage. Thus, *eante hōs on . . . ante hōs mē on* now expresses the recommendation to derive results from supposing one's original hypothesis to obtain, and again to derive results from supposing that one's original hypothesis does not obtain. The original hypothesis and its negation will each be applied to derive results for *all* the things in all the relations specified in 136c1–3.

Let us evaluate this reading in its turn. The only difficulty I can see for it is that it takes the occurrences of *ontos* that appear in 136b7 to have a different use from those of *on* in 136c4. (It takes the occurrences of *ontos* in the sense of *is,* and those of *on* in the sense of *is the case.*) But this is clearly possible, and will I think be acceptable when we observe this reading's advantages. Reading II solves the problems associated with the mysterious third antecedent, restoring the symmetry between the two groups of sections of arguments. We may also note that it is desirable to give three possible forms the original hypothesis can take, as this reading (among others) does. For the method when understood in this way is generally applicable to any claim that can be put in subject-predicate form, and not just to existence claims. This prevents the reference to the joint project of the Eleatics and their opponents from being totally inapposite. The claims with which they are said to have dealt are not here phrased as existence claims. Rather, we get: *ei polla esti ta onta* ("if the things that are are many," 127e1–2) and *hen phēis einai to pan* ("You say the all is one," 128a8–b1).

Moreover, the general plan of the exercise on Reading II is now very close to that in the particular case of the exercise starting from Zeno's hypothesis. It may be convenient to compare the two descriptions as follows:

Ordering of Reading II

I. If the original hypothesis obtains, what follows for the subject in relation to itself.

II. If the original hypothesis obtains, what follows for the subject in relation to the others.

III. If the original hypothesis obtains, what follows for the others in relation to themselves.

IV. If the original hypothesis obtains, what follows for the others in relation to the subject.

V. If the original hypothesis does not obtain, what follows for the subject in relation to itself.

VI. If the original hypothesis does not obtain, what follows for the subject in relation to the others.

VII. If the original hypothesis does not obtain, what follows for the others in relation to themselves.

VIII. If the original hypothesis does not obtain, what follows for the others in relation to the subject.

Zeno's Hypothesis as an Example

I. On the hypothesis of the being of The Many, what follows for The Many in relation to themselves.

II. On the hypothesis of the being of The Many, what follows for The Many in relation to The One.

III. On the hypothesis of the being of The Many, what follows for The One in relation to itself.

IV. On the hypothesis of the being of The Many, what follows for The One in relation to The Many.

V. On the hypothesis of the nonbeing of The Many, what follows for The One in relation to itself.

VI. On the hypothesis of the nonbeing of The Many, what follows for The One in relation to The Many.

VII. On the hypothesis of the nonbeing of The Many, what follows for The Many in relation to themselves.

VIII. On the hypothesis of the nonbeing of The Many, what follows for The Many in relation to The One.[7]

Clearly, understanding the general description of the exercise according to Reading II gives the general and particular descriptions a high degree of similarity. (The only departure from complete similarity occurs because of an irregularity within the description of the particular case: when describing the results from the negative hypothesis there, results for The One are mentioned before those for The Many, even though the subject in this case is The Many. Such minor variations from the rule as there are can be understood as tolerable because unimportant.) Consideration of the general description's relation to the particular descriptions thus joins with reflection on the internal coher-

ence of the general description in indicating that we should prefer
Reading II.

The overall structure of the recommended exercise has now emerged
clearly: its first half consists in four sections of results from an original
hypothesis, and its second half is made up of four sections of results
from the negation of the original hypothesis. The descriptions of the
individual sections of argument are generated as follows: each section
is described by one of the eight possible combinations of one each
from the following three pairs: *If the positive hypothesis obtains / If
its negation does, what follows for the subject / for the others*, and *in
relation to itself / in relation to the others*.

Everything that we have done so far in considering the structure of
the proposed exercise has involved considering the coherence of the
transitional section. Having obtained a reading of the general description that restores that coherence, we can now take up the issue of what
one might call the "fit" between the transitional section and the second part of the dialogue. A feature of the editions of Burnet and Diès,
as I remarked at the beginning of this chapter, is the incompatibility
of Parmenides' methodological remarks with the display he gives to
demonstrate the method. I will first show (briefly) that the second part
of the dialogue does not match any of the plans outlined by the four
possible readings based on their editions. I will then show that the
repunctuation and Reading II yield a plan that the second part of the
dialogue does match. This will, I think, complete the case in favor of
Reading II.

To make the proposed comparisons we need a characterization of
the sections of argument that appear in the second part of the dialogue.
Because the sections of argument are marked off by brief openings
and closings, detailed study of the arguments themselves is not needed.
We can obtain a provisional characterization that will serve our present
purpose by consulting the openings of the sections in question (137c4,
142b1–5, 157b6–8, 159b2–5, 160b5–6, 163b7–c1, 164b5–6, 165e2–
3). These openings allow us to identify eight sections,[8] of which the
first four derive results from a positive hypothesis, while the last four
do so from a negative one.

We can see very quickly that this pattern of sections diverges con-
siderably from that prescribed by the first four readings of the general
description of the exercise. On Reading Ia, the exercise is to consist

of only four sections of argument—that is, the description on this reading is adequate to only *half* of what we actually get. This reading only mentions one hypothesis, instead of a positive hypothesis and a negative one. Reading Ib on the other hand prescribes too many sections, ten. Also, the ordering of the sections on Reading Ib is very different from that in the second part of the dialogue; whereas Ib listed all results for the subject first, and then all results for the others, the second part has first all results from the positive hypothesis, and then all those from the negative one. On Reading Ic, this gross feature of the ordering is wrong in the same way; all results for the subject are given before any of those for the others. The number of sections is incorrect on this reading too: it generates only six. Finally, Reading Id yields the greatest number of sections, recommending twelve. And the order is incorrect in the familiar way: its first six sections derive results for the subject and its final six do so for the others.

Let us now turn to Reading II. As is clear from either the paraphrase of the passage or from the listing of the sections (which I made to compare with the plan of the exercise in the case of Zeno's hypothesis), the passage on Reading II outlines an exercise consisting in eight sections, of which the first four are to be devoted to deriving results from some chosen hypothesis, and the last four to deriving results from the negation of the original hypothesis. That is, Reading II alone of all those considered yields a scheme compatible with our preliminary characterization of the actual exercise. Taking this together with the result already obtained, that Reading II alone made the methodological remarks coherent, I now regard this reading as being sufficiently confirmed and recommend repunctuating the passage accordingly.[9]

In adopting Reading II, we have answered the first of the two questions I listed as forming the program for this chapter: we have determined the structure of the exercise Parmenides recommends. That is, we now have a characterization of the exercise that tells us, *given a hypothesis,* what sections of results to derive. We can now consider the choice of hypothesis that is to be the starting point for the actual demonstration Parmenides gives.

At first this hardly seems to admit of question. Parmenides raises the issue explicitly and states his hypothesis as follows:

πόθεν οὖν δὴ ἀρξόμεθα καὶ τί πρῶτον ὑποθησόμεθα; ἢ βού-
λεσθε . . . ἀπ᾽ ἐμαυτοῦ ἄρξωμαι καὶ τῆς ἐμαυτοῦ ὑποθέσεως,
περὶ τοῦ ἑνὸς αὐτοῦ ὑποθέμενος, εἴτε ἕν ἐστιν εἴτε μὴ ἕν, τί χρὴ
συμβαίνειν; (137a7–b4)

Well, now, where shall we start from, and what shall we hypothesize
first? Do you wish . . . me to start from myself and from my own
hypothesis, hypothesizing about The One itself,[10] ****, what must follow?

As I stated at the opening of this chapter, I regard the section of the
received text whose place is held in the translation by the asterisks as
problematic. As candidates to go in place of the asterisks, we will
need to consider three possible renderings:

    (a) if The One is or if The One is not
    (b) if it is one or if it is not one
    (c) if The One is or if The Not-One is.

A summary of the advantages and disadvantages associated with each
of these three translations of the received text will be useful before we
turn to a more detailed discussion.

Reading (c) is an easy sense for the words in question to bear, but
it goes against our understanding of the structure of the exercise (the
second member of the pair of hypotheses ought to be the negation of
the first one). It also fails to match the actual demonstration Parmenides gives. It has, as far as I know, had no advocates, and I think we
may safely dispense with it now.

Reading (b) also emerges easily from the text and does yield the
right relation between the positive and negative hypotheses. But it has
an enormous drawback: it, too, fails to match the actual exercise.

Reading (a) matches the actual exercise, as well as yielding the right
relation between the positive and negative hypotheses. But (a) is very
strained as a reading of the received text (indeed, I think, impossible).
It has recently obtained the support of R. E. Allen in his translation
and analysis of the *Parmenides*. But Allen's lengthy discussion addresses only the issue of why the hypotheses *ought to be* as given in (a);
he does not even attempt to show that the received text can bear this
meaning (nor is the passage he cites in Robinson helpful).[11]

I offer a new discussion. (I take it that one point on which I relied
just now, that the second member of the pair of hypotheses should be

the negation of the first member of the pair, has already been established.) First, I will collect the evidence that shows that (b) fails to match the actual display Parmenides gives, whereas (a) does match it. Next, I will explain why the received text yields only (b) naturally. Finally, I will indicate a resolution of the situation. A very small emendation can give us a corrected text which yields (a), the desired reading, unambiguously.

To see what hypotheses are used in the actual exercise, we need only consult the openings of the sections of argument. Some are themselves ambiguous. For example, in 137c4 we find:

εἰ ἕν ἐστιν.

Here, *hen* could be the subject of *estin,* yielding: if The One is. But, equally, it could be taken as a complement, so that we would have: if it is one. But we do find one opening statement that cannot be ambiguous. The passage 160b5–6 reads:

εἰ δὲ δὴ μὴ ἔστι τὸ ἕν, τί χρὴ συμβαίνειν ἆρ᾽ οὐ σκεπτέον μετὰ τοῦτο;

Because the definite article appears before *hen* here, this cannot mean:

. . . if it is not one . . .

It is most naturally [12] rendered as:

. . . if The One is not . . .

The circumstance that the hypothesis is restated immediately after, at 160b6–7, as *ei hen mē estin* shows that the formulation lacking the article is not meant to bear any different meaning from that with it. (Nor ought it to, since, as we have already established, the same negative hypothesis ought to be used all four times.) Given that the negative hypothesis used in this section must be

If The One is not,

and that in generating sections of argument the same positive hypothesis is to be used four times, and then its negation in turn is to be used four times, we can now conclude [13] that the hypotheses actually used in the second part of the dialogue are:

If The One is

and

If The One is not.

This pair of hypotheses is plainly not the pair recommended according to rendering (b) of 137b4; it is the pair yielded by rendering (a).

Now we need to determine what the received text at 137b4

εἴτε ἕν ἐστιν εἴτε μὴ ἕν

can yield without being tortured. If we consider on its own the phrase

εἰ ἕν ἐστιν

there are two ways of construing it. *Hen* could be the predicate, yielding:

If it is one.

But, equally, *hen* could be the subject. The hypothesis would then be:

If The One is.

On the other hand, in the case of the negative hypothesis

εἰ μὴ ἕν

it seems to me that the two construals are very far from being on an equal footing with each other. It seems overwhelmingly natural to take this as:

If it is not one.

Because the negative particle appears directly before the word for one, whereas the word for is has to be supplied,[14] it is most natural to take "one" as what is being negated. The other reading advocated seems extremely strained. It translates this phrase as:

If The One is not.

But this requires us not only to supply "is," but to detach the negative particle from the word it does appear with and understand it as going rather with the "is" (which we have supplied).

At this point we may make an observation that will allow us to avoid the tedium of considering all the combinations of each of the two construals that I just introduced for each of the two phrases. We must construe them both *in the same way* (i.e., we must take *hen* as the subject in both phrases, or as the predicate in both). Anything else would be violently unnatural. Moreover, the parallelism of the two phrases is guaranteed by our understanding of the structure of the exercise: the negative hypothesis must be the negation of the positive one. This leaves us with our two candidate readings:

(a) if The One is or if The One is not

and

(b) if it is one or if it is not one.

Reading (a), if tenable at all, is only barely so, its untenability being due to its extremely strained rendering of the second phrase.

The intrinsic implausibility of reading (a) as an understanding of the received text is increased by two additional considerations. First, there are less misleading ways of saying

If The One is or if The One is not

in Greek that Plato could have used if he had this interpretation in mind. Also, there is the matter of the influence of the context on the understanding of our present passage. Parmenides here says that he is starting from his own hypothesis of The One (137b3–4). And we already have some information from Socrates' exchange with Zeno concerning what Parmenides was doing. Socrates said there (without Parmenides or Zeno objecting) *hen phēis einai to pan* ("you say the all is one," 128a8–b1). That context seems to me to determine (if it needed any further determination) that a reader coming to the phrase

εἴτε ἕν ἐστιν εἴτε μὴ ἕν

would, at that point in his reading, take it in the sense of: "If it is one or if it is not one." This would connect satisfactorily with the earlier information about Parmenides' project in a way in which "If The One is or if the One is not" would not. We can now conclude, therefore, that the context interacts with Parmenides' announcement to determine that the hypotheses to be used *according to the received text* would be those given by reading (b):

If it is one

and

If it is not one.

However, only the slightest of emendations is needed to remedy matters. One could simply bracket the second *hen* in 137b4, leaving:

εἴτε ἓν ἔστιν εἴτε μή

If The One is or not.

This would naturally be taken to be a short way of saying:

If The One is or if The One is not.

Alternatively, one could replace the second *hen* with *estin,* and read

εἴτε ἓν ἔστιν εἴτε μὴ ἔστιν

which also has the desired sense: If The One is or is not. Since this is followed by *ti chrē sumbainein,* the second *estin* could have been changed to *hen* easily. For the change in question is from ΜΗΕΣΤΙΝΤΙ to ΜΗΕΝΤΙ. We need only suppose that ΣΤΙ dropped out, which is not difficult.

Although I originally considered these conjectures independently, they in fact have some authority. Max Wundt proposed the same two possible corrections, and they were accepted by Cornford.[15] Wundt's discussion is confined to a footnote and is very brief. Evidently, his main motivation was to make Parmenides' announcement here match his actual display in the second half of the dialogue. The reading of the received text he saw as natural was (c), so that he proposed his conjecture as an alternative to it rather than (as I have been doing) to (b). In any case, what we need to do now is to revive these suggestions. Each change is modest, but brings with it a major improvement: instead of announcing that he is proceeding from one pair of hypotheses but then in practice using a different pair, Parmenides in the corrected text states the pair of hypotheses that he does use. For with either correction, we get Parmenides announcing that he will take as his pair of hypotheses:

If The One is

and

If The One is not.

This matches the openings of the arguments that come in the second part of the dialogue. Also, since the text so corrected yields the desired sense unambiguously, it is immune to the influence of the earlier description of Parmenides' activity.[16]

We have now determined the general scheme of the exercise, as well as the starting point from which, in the second part of the dialogue, Parmenides will derive his results. But these determinations are purely formal. We can make lists of the kinds of sections of argument we expect, but we have no real understanding of the descriptions of those sections. To develop a satisfactory understanding of those descriptions, we will have to make sense of the "in-relation-to" qualifications that figure so prominently in them. That is the task of the next chapter.

3

The In-Relation-To
Qualifications

Obviously, the results of chapter 2, by themselves, do not enable us
to understand the new kind of exercise completely. We can understand
abstractly that the deriving of results from both positive and negative
hypotheses allows us to "see what difference" the state of affairs we
hypothesize makes. We can also understand that by deriving results
for the others as well as for the subject of the hypotheses we broaden
our field of observation. (In fact, it seems that there would not automatically be substantive results for the others from any claim about
any subject. Thus, if such results follow, that is itself a significant fact
about the subject's role in the world.)

However, the total obscurity of the "in-relation-to" qualifications
("in relation to itself" and "in relation to the others") makes it impossible fully to grasp the description of even a single section of results within the Parmenidean dialectic. One or the other of the pair is
employed in describing each section of the exercise, yet the purpose
this serves is not obvious, and the methodological remarks give us no
guidance in the matter. We can now appreciate the interest of the
remaining question, which is reserved for the present chapter: What is
the force of the in-relation-to qualifications?[1] Answering this question
will go a long way in helping us to understand Parmenides' new kind
of dialectic. Indeed, looking at the matter from a slightly different
angle, we might think that Plato's purpose in describing the exercise
in terms that stress these mysterious qualifications so laboriously is
actually to draw our attention to the importance of working out the
distinction they indeed mark.

Exploring the in-relation-to qualifications will be the program of this
chapter. I will first confirm that these qualifications do pertain to the

arguments of the second part of the dialogue. (So far, the expectation that they do has been based on a study of the transitional methodological remarks alone.) Next, I will consider the preposition *pros* with the accusative (the relevant construction). This will prepare us for the main task of the chapter—determining the force of Plato's in-relation-to qualifications—by making it clear exactly what information we need to obtain from Parmenides' display.

My study of constructions with *pros* will in fact enable me to identify suggestive occurrences of the construction in the course of the arguments; this will result in my determination of the force of *pros ta alla* (in relation to the others). That done, I will be in a position to make progress in understanding the import of the qualification *pros heauto* (in relation to itself). Since I will by then have exhausted explicit occurrences of the word *pros,*[2] I will bring to the inquiry two tenets that I have already developed: that the arguments and their conclusions should be understood in such a way as to be acceptable (chapter 1), and that the first section derives results for the subject in relation to itself (this arises out of the discussion in chapter 2 of the ordering of the recommended sections). I will concentrate on arguments from this first group that seem to involve mistakes when read without qualification, and then develop an understanding of the in-relation-to-itself qualification such that the arguments construed with its help can at last be recognized to be reasonable.

The in-relation-to qualifications, as I understand them, will turn out to mark a distinction between two kinds of predication. This distinction is in fact the key innovation of the *Parmenides,* ultimately making it possible for Plato to avoid the problems of the immature Socrates of the first part of the dialogue. Because of the importance of the distinction for interpreting the dialogue and for tracing the development of Plato's thought, it will be desirable to be as clear as possible about the distinction itself. For this reason, I will conclude this chapter with some exploration of the two kinds of predication.

Confirmation of the Role of the In-Relation-To Qualifications

In chapter 2, information found in the second part of the dialogue confirmed my assertions (based on Parmenides' methodological remarks) concerning the number of sections of argument to be produced, and the character of the hypotheses to be used in generating those sections. I obtained this information independently of study of the arguments themselves by considering the opening and closing remarks that separate the sections of argument. It is desirable to get confirmation also of the assertion that the in-relation-to qualifications contribute to the structure of the second part of the dialogue.

In fact, the mere appearance of eight sections[3] of argument is confirmation of a kind. For let us suppose that the only specifications relevant were: *If the original claim holds / If it does not,* and *what follows for the subject / for the others.* In this case, there would be only four descriptions consisting of one member from each pair of the relevant specifications. On the other hand, the combinations (one from each pair) of the elements of three pairs of specifications yield eight section-descriptions. And if some third pair of specifications is in play in generating the sections of argument, it is likely to be the one Plato himself used in describing the exercise in the methodological remarks; that is, it is likely to be the pair of specifications now under study: *in relation to itself / in relation to the others.* However, this consideration should be supplemented by some more explicit indication of the role of this third pair of specifications.

The openings of the sections contain no such indications. Each opening makes explicit that the section it introduces starts from either the positive or the negative hypothesis, and derives results either for The One or for the others; however, these openings do not employ the third pair of specifications. This may have been the cause of people's losing sight of the importance of the specifications. To see that this is a mistake, we need only consider the *closing* remarks of the sections. In particular, it is the closing of the fourth and eighth sections of arguments that are relevant now. These are important because of the combination of their function with their position. Each of these two closings undertakes to summarize all that has been established in the exercise up to that point. Thus, one undertakes to tell in brief what has been accomplished by the first half of the dialectic, and the other presents the results of the entire thirty-page exercise. They run as follows:

Οὕτω δὴ ἓν εἰ ἔστιν, πάντα τέ ἐστι τὸ ἓν καὶ οὐδὲ ἕν ἐστι καὶ πρὸς ἑαυτὸ καὶ πρὸς τἆλλα, καὶ τἆλλα ὡσαύτως. (160b2–3)[4]

Thus if The One is, The One is everything and not even one in relation to itself and in relation to the others, and the others similarly.

Εἰρήσθω τοίνυν τοῦτό τε καὶ ὅτι, ὡς ἔοικεν, ἓν εἴτ᾽ ἔστιν εἴτε μὴ ἔστιν, αὐτό τε καὶ τἆλλα καὶ πρὸς αὑτὰ καὶ πρὸς ἄλληλα πάντα πάντως ἐστί τε καὶ οὐκ ἔστι καὶ φαίνεταί τε καὶ οὐ φαίνεται. (166c2–5)

Let this be said therefore, and that, as it appears, if The One is or is not, it and the others in relation to themselves and in relation to each other are all things in all ways and are not, and seem and seem not.

Despite the highly compressed and schematic character of these summaries, they both employ the in-relation-to qualifications. The appearance of these phrases in important summaries that reduce the results of the exercise to their barest outlines shows Plato assigned an ineliminable role to this mysterious pair of specifications.

Thus in this case as in the others, expectations derived from our interpretation of the methodological remarks have been confirmed by evidence taken from the second part of the dialogue. That is, we have now confirmed that the in-relation-to qualifications do pertain to the sections of argument constituting Parmenides' dialectical display. Now we need to develop an understanding of how the qualifications function, and in what way they apply to the arguments.

How the Construction Functions

As a first step in determining the force of the specifications *in relation to itself* and *in relation to the others*, I will analyze the way in which *pros* with the accusative (the relevant construction) functions in Greek. This will help us to realize what we should look for when we turn to the actual arguments that constitute Parmenides' demonstration.

Grammarians and lexicographers[5] give a rather general equivalent for *pros* with the accusative: in relation to (or with reference to). But they also give an array of much more specific glosses, including among many others: toward (hostile), toward (in a nonhostile sense), at (time), compared with, and suitably to. This group looks extremely diverse, and it at first seems strange that a single word could have such an array of independent meanings. In fact, as the availability of the gen-

eral translation (in relation to) suggests, there is no array of independent meanings. Rather, as we will see in what follows, it is possible
to regard the word (in this construction) as always having the same
core function: that of signaling relationality. More specific glosses become appropriate as a result of the interaction between this core function and the context of use. That is, the context determines what the
relation is whose obtaining *pros* (in relation to) indicates, and this may
make some one of the many particular translations appropriate.

It will be much easier to see this if we look at some examples. I
have chosen for analysis some of the passages cited in Smyth's grammar and the lexicon of Liddell, Scott, and Jones (LSJ). Let us start
with:

εἰ δέ τινος ἔτι ἐνδεῖσθαι δοκεῖτε, πρὸς ἐμὲ λέγετε· (Xenophon,
Cyropaedia 6.4.19)

And if something still seems to you to be lacking, speak *to (pros)* me.

Here, we could adopt the stilted translation of *pros eme legete:* "speak
in relation to (pros) me." The reason this is so stilted is that *legein*
(speak) is itself the relation whose obtaining *pros* (the relationality
marker) indicates. The briefer "speak to me" conveys this less heavily
than the stilted translation. In this case, since *legete* ("speak") occurs
in the sentence, there is no need for any notions not explicitly named
to be supplied. If *pros* were always used in this way, it would be no
more than a syntactic aid in the use of relational predicates.

But the use of *pros* is not so confined. It can indicate the obtaining
(and bearing on whatever the rest of the sentence is asserting) of some
relation that is *not itself named in the sentence.* The relation in question will then be indicated by the context as appropriate, and the range
of relations that contexts can manage to specify is the source of the
range of the particular glosses on *pros* with which we started. Let us
look, for example, at:

πρὸς ὧν δὴ τοῦτο τὸ κήρυγμα οὔτε τίς οἱ διαλέγεσθαι οὔτε οἱ-
κίοισι δέκεσθαι ἤθελε·(Herodotus 3.52)

As a result of (pros) this proclamation, no one was willing to speak
with him or to receive him at home.

Although *dialegesthai* (speak with) and *dekesthai* (receive) are relational predicates, their relata are filled in independently of the *pros*

construction. What the *pros* construction does rather is introduce something further in connection with the assertion "no one was willing to speak with him or to receive him at home." It tells us that what is asserted has some relation to a proclamation. The context makes clear that the relation in question is causal: it is because of the proclamation that no one was willing to speak to the person in question. So, the core function of *pros* (indicating relationality) here interacts with the context to produce the translation "as a result of the proclamation." Although this context makes clear that the relation whose obtaining *pros* indicates is casual, this is by no means the only sort of relation that can be so indicated.

We find a comparative relation indicated by *pros* in Thucydides' famous remark (1.10—I use Smith's translation from the Loeb edition, italics and *"pros"* added) concerning the disparity between the glory of the Spartans and their architectural achievements:

Λακεδαιμονίων μὲν γὰρ εἰ ἡ πόλις ἐρημωθείη, λειφθείη δὲ τά τε ἱερὰ καὶ τῆς κατασκευῆς τὰ ἐδάφη, πολλὴν ἂν οἶμαι ἀπιστίαν τῆς δυνάμεως προσελθόντος πολλοῦ χρόνου τοῖς ἔπειτα *πρὸς* τὸ κλέος αὐτῶν εἶναι. . .

For if the city of the Lacedaemonians should be deserted, and nothing should be left of it but its temples and the foundations of its other buildings, posterity would, I think, after a long lapse of time, be very loath to believe that their power was *as great as (pros)* their renown.

Here the basic notion is that people under the imagined conditions would have great disbelief in the power of the Spartans. What the *pros* construction adds is an indication of some relation that bears on the imagined disbelief: it is a disbelief in the power of the Spartans *in comparison with* their fame—that is, people who see architectural remains as significant will not be able to believe that the real power of the Spartans bears comparison with their reputation. That the relation in question is comparative becomes explicit in Hobbes's translation (italics and *"pros"* added): "I think it would breed much unbelief in posterity long hence, of their power, *in comparison of (pros)* the fame."

Let us now turn to Aristotle's *Rhetoric* 1367a32:

ἐλευθέρου γὰρ τὸ μὴ *πρὸς* ἄλλον ζῆν.

For it belongs to a free man not to live *with reference to (pros)* another.

Here the infinitive *zēn* obviously does not name the relation signaled by *pros* ("live" is not even a relational predicate). Nor is Aristotle saying that the free man has nothing to do with others (has *no relations* with them). But there is some relation to others that Aristotle thinks is not fitting for a free man. Evidently it is having his actions *determined by* them.

A somewhat similar relation is indicated in Aristotle's remark at *Politics* 1310a14 that what most contributes to the permanence of constitutions is:

τὸ παιδεύεσθαι πρὸς τὰς πολιτείας.

⟨people's⟩ being educated *suitably to (pros)* their constitutions.

We can again say that the *pros* construction indicates *some relation* as being recommended between people's educations and their constitutions (or regimes). Given that we are talking of preserving the constitutions, it becomes obvious that the relation in question (as LSJ suggests) is suitability.

A third use of this kind occurs in Demosthenes 15.28:

ὁρῶ . . . ἅπαντας πρὸς τὴν παροῦσαν δύναμιν τῶν δικαίων ἀξιουμένους.

I see . . . all men making their claims of right *according to (pros)* their present power.

Here as often, the stilted use of the general equivalent for *pros* is almost viable as a translation, yielding:

I see all men making their claims of right *in relation to (pros)* their present power.

But here as often, such a translation is unacceptably unnatural, because it is so obvious what the relation in question is. Hence natural translations incorporate this information, yielding "according to their power."

Let us now sum all this up in terms of the general schema:

A is B *pros* C

A is B in relation to C.

We have seen that this construction may be used to indicate that B itself is the relation holding between A and C. But it may also be used in case some relation to C *not necessarily named* is relevant to A's being B (a causal relation, a comparative relation, a relation of suitability, etc.) In such cases, the kinds of things A, B, and C happen to be, or other elements of the context, determine what the relation in question is.

Let us now apply this to our thinking about the in-relation-to qualifications used in the *Parmenides*. To take one member of the pair as an example, we can see that constructions of the form

A is B *pros ta alla*

A is B in relation to the others

could be used to indicate that B is a relation holding between A and the others. But we can also see that this is not the only way the construction can be used: it could also indicate that some relation to the others *that we need to identify* is relevant to A's being B.

We can now turn to the text of the *Parmenides,* prepared with the thought that what we need to do is to discover what relations Plato may have in mind when he speaks of finding consequences for something "in relation to itself" and "in relation to the others." I shall start by considering two interpretations of these phrases that need to be considered but can be rejected on fairly general grounds. I will then proceed to develop my own views about the qualifications by thinking carefully about particular arguments from the second part of the dialogue.

Two Interpretations Eliminated

Many of the occurrences of the word *pros* with the accusative in the second part of the dialogue are in the type of construction in which

A is B *pros* C

A is B in relation to C

indicates that relation B holds between A and C. That is, we find *pros* occurring frequently as a syntactic aid in the use of relational predicates. So a possibility that needs to be disposed of is that the *pros heauto/pros ta alla* distinction reflects some sorting based on a grouping together of relational predicates. By "relational predicates" I mean the familiar group including: is the double of, is the niece of, is taller than. This contrasts with a nonrelational group including: is blue, is round, is a stone.

The two interpretations I will dispose of first are two ways of developing this idea. The first is to suppose that the specification *pros ta alla* (in relation to the others) selects results whose statement involves relational predicates, whereas the specification *pros heauto* (in relation to itself) selects results in terms of nonrelational predicates. That is, the distinction according to this interpretation is *between* relational and nonrelational predicates. The second way of developing the idea is to suppose that results *pros ta alla* (in relation to the others) give relations that hold between the subject and the others, whereas results *pros heauto* (in relation to itself) give relations that hold between the subject and itself. On this view the distinction is *within* the group of relational predicates.

The first way of developing the idea is to suppose that all the results involving relational predicates are the results *pros ta alla*, whereas the results involving nonrelational predicates are *pros heauto*. There could be some reason to characterize the results involving relational predicates (traditionally called *pros ti*, after all) as *pros ta alla*, to emphasize that the grammatical complement or second term in the relation (whose place is held by *ti* in the phrase *pros ti*) is generally something other than the subject. *Pros heauto* as a name for the nonrelational type would have to be taken as a back-formation, gesturing somewhat inappositely at the type's more intrinsic character. Such a construal is rather strained, which is a mark against this interpretation from the start.

To continue testing it, we may observe that, when combined with Parmenides' statement of the structure of the dialectical exercise, this interpretation of the in-relation-to qualifications predicts that four of the recommended sections of argument establish results in terms of relational predicates, whereas the other four deal in nonrelational predicates. Brief reflection shows that this idea lacks merit. First of all, the same list of predicates is in question in each of the eight sections of argument.[6] So there is no difference between the lists of predicates in question in different sections that the relational/nonrelational distinction could hope to capture. Moreover, this canonical list combines predicates that the distinction now under consideration regards as relational (e.g., being equal and unequal to) with others that are not *pros ti* in this sense (e.g., being one, having being, being at rest).

The first mark against this preliminary attempt at interpreting the *pros heauto/pros ta alla* distinction was that it took *pros heauto* (literally: in relation to itself) as meaning: not really relationally after all. It is clearly better to take the hint of the surface grammar and accept that results *pros heauto* are importantly relational. The second interpretation I wish to reject takes the hint in the most simpleminded way. According to this idea, sections whose results could be schematized

A is B *pros ta alla*

would tell us which relations B held between A and the others, whereas those with results of the form

A is B *pros heauto*

would report on relations B obtaining between A and itself. It is obvious that this second interpretation will not succeed either. For it predicts that a *pros heauto* section will consider only reflexive relations, whereas one *pros ta alla* will deal in relations between its subject and other things. Thus, a *pros heauto* section might tell us that its subject is identical with itself, the same age as itself, and so on, whereas one *pros ta alla* would indicate that its subject is greater than some things, to the left of others, and so on. This does not fit the text at all, nor does it seem likely that the production of such results arranged as in Parmenides' scheme would be philosophically fruitful.

What the failure of these first two interpretations shows is that the import of each of the in-relation-to qualifications in the schematic formulations (which represent in general form the results obtained in the course of the exercise)

A is B *pros heauto*

A is B *pros ta alla*

has nothing to do with the relationality or lack of it of B. That is, the distinction in question is neither to separate results in which the predicate B is nonrelational from those in which the predicate B is relational, nor to separate results in which the relation B holds between the

subject and itself from those in which the relation B holds between the
subject and the others.

We rather find ourselves dealing with uses of the in-relation-to construction as more than a syntactic aid for relational predicates. Our
uses are of the kind in which the in-relation-to construction brings in
some new element that bears on the fact that A is B. That is,

A is B *pros heauto*

indicates that *some relation as yet unnamed* to the subject bears on
A's being B. Similarly,

A is B *pros ta alla*

indicates that *some relation as yet unknown* to the others bears on A's
being B. This opens up the possibility that some philosophically interesting relations may be involved. We can now notice that the difference in force between "in relation to itself" and "in relation to the
others" need not be due only to the contrast between "itself" and
"the others." For each expression indicates the bearing of an unnamed relation, and we have no reason to expect the relation in question to be common to both. In fact, my study will show that two
different relations are indicated, and this fact is crucial in determining
the different force of the two in-relation-to qualifications. Moreover,
since they in fact mark a difference between two kinds of predication,
a single form of words "A is B" will often have different truth conditions depending on whether it is made as a predication *pros heauto*
or as a predication *pros ta alla*. What we need to do now is to discover
how to understand the in-relation-to qualifications. To do this, I will
start with occurrences of *pros* that suggest the obtaining of an unnamed relation.

Predication *Pros ta Alla*

I would now like to draw attention to some occurrences of the word
pros in the fifth section of arguments. Because we have become aware
of how crucial the context is, I will give the passages in which we
find these occurrences. The first passage contains two occurrences of
pros. Comparing them will be of special interest to us. It runs as
follows:

Καὶ ἀνομοιότης ἄρα ἐστὶν αὐτῷ πρὸς τὰ ἄλλα· τὰ γὰρ ἄλλα τοῦ ἑνὸς ἕτερα ὄντα ἑτεροῖα καὶ εἴη ἄν.—Ναί.—Τὰ δ' ἑτεροῖα οὐκ ἀλλοῖα;—Πῶς δ' οὔ;—Τὰ δ' ἀλλοῖα οὐκ ἀνόμοια;—Ἀνόμοια μὲν οὖν.—Οὐκοῦν εἴπερ τῷ ἑνὶ ἀνόμοιά ἐστι, δῆλον ὅτι ἀνομοίῳ τά γε ἀνόμοια ἀνόμοια ἂν εἴη.—Δῆλον.—Εἴη δὴ ἂν καὶ τῷ ἑνὶ ἀνομοιότης, πρὸς ἣν τὰ ἄλλα ἀνόμοια αὐτῷ ἐστιν.—Ἔοικεν. (161a6–b4)

And ⟨The One⟩ has Unlikeness in relation to *(pros)* the others. For the others being different from The One would be different in kind.—Yes.— And aren't things different in kind other in kind?—How not?—And aren't things other in kind unlike?—They are unlike.—Accordingly, if indeed they are unlike The One, it is clear that the unlike things would be unlike to an unlike thing.—It is clear.—Then The One would have Unlikeness, in relation to *(pros)* which the others are unlike it.—So it seems.

I will give the second passage now, since the similarity of the passages for present purposes will make separate discussion unnecessary.

Τὰ δὲ μὴ ἴσα οὐκ ἄνισα;—Ναί.—Τὰ δὲ ἄνισα οὐ τῷ ἀνίσῳ ἄνισα;—Πῶς δ' οὔ;—Καὶ ἀνισότητος δὴ μετέχει τὸ ἕν, πρὸς ἣν τἆλλα αὐτῷ ἐστιν ἄνισα;—Μετέχει. (161c7–d1)

Aren't things not equal unequal?—Yes.—And aren't unequal things unequal to an unequal thing?—How not?—Then The One has a share of Inequality, in relation to *(pros)* which the others are unequal to it?—It does have a share.

When we read 161a6–b4 we first notice that the basic purpose of the argument is to establish that The One will have Unlikeness, if The One is not. The argument moves directly from the fact that The One is unlike the others to the conclusion that The One has Unlikeness. This must rely on some background thoughts that demand that The One cannot be unlike the others without Unlikeness having something to do with it. However, we are not yet ready to analyze that step in the argument. Our immediate purpose is to compare the uses of *pros* in the two statements of the argument's conclusion. One precedes and one follows the argument; the alternate wording of the second statement is most significant. The two statements are:

Καὶ ἀνομοιότης ἄρα ἐστὶν αὐτῷ πρὸς τὰ ἄλλα· (161a6)

And ⟨The One⟩ has Unlikeness in relation to *(pros)* the others

and

Εἴη δὴ ἂν καὶ τῷ ἑνὶ ἀνομοιότης, πρὸς ἣν τὰ ἄλλα ἀνόμοια αὐτῷ
ἐστιν. (161b3–4)

Then The One would have Unlikeness, in relation to *(pros)* which the
others are unlike it.

When we look only at the first statement, we find the familiar use
of *pros* as a syntactic aid in the use of relational predicates, which has
already proved irrelevant to our inquiry. But there is a crucial difference between the two statements. Although both refer to Unlikeness,
the others, and The One, in the first statement The One has Unlikeness
pros the others, whereas in the second statement the others are unlike
The One *pros* Unlikeness. Clearly, *pros* does not introduce the same
relation in both occurrences. Suppose someone asks: "But in relation
to *what* is it unlike?" The two answers "in relation to the others"
and "in relation to Unlikeness" are not only different but of different sorts.
If these two are sufficiently different, the second may be useful to us,
even if the first is not.

One way to see what kind of difference there is between the two
statements is to consider some manipulations. We can see intuitively
that while

(1) The One is unlike *pros* the others

(2) The others are unlike *pros* The One

and

(3) The One and the others are unlike

are all equivalent;

(4) The One is unlike *pros* Unlikeness

is not equivalent to

(5) Unlikeness is unlike *pros* The One

and is certainly not equivalent to

(6) The One and Unlikeness are unlike.

We can now analyze what lies behind these intuitions, in terms of
our previous observations concerning the variety of uses that construc-

tions with the preposition *pros* can have. Clearly, in (1) the relation *pros* signals is Unlikeness. That is, (1) exemplifies the special case in which the sentence's own predicate is not only relational, but is the relation whose obtaining *pros* indicates. (This is of course the type of occurrence that we have already determined to be unimportant for our inquiry.) Other examples would be:

(7) Dion is kind *pros* Theon

(8) Dion spoke *pros* Theon

(in contexts that make it clear that Theon is the person to whom Dion is kind, and spoke). Because the kindness relation is the one *pros* introduces in (7), it is permissible to write:

Kind (Dion, Theon).

Similarly, in the general case, where the *pros* in

R (A) *pros* C

indicates R itself as the relation obtaining between A and C, we may write

R (A, C)

and go on to its equivalent

R* (C, A)

(where R* is the inverse relation to R). This is what lies behind our intuition that (1) is equivalent to (2) and (3).

But as the nonequivalence of (4) to (5) and (6) hints, (4) is clearly a different kind of case from (1). This is a sign of the fact that (4) belongs to the group in which the relation *pros* indicates is not named in the sentence at all. Close parallels to (4) would be:

(9) A is kind *pros* Kindness

(10) B is a tree *pros* Treehood.

When we consider (9) (if we imagine it occurring in a context in which it is useful and true), it is obvious that the sentence is not telling us that the kindness relation holds between A and Kindness—that is, it is not telling us that A is *kind to* Kindness. Rather, (9) is true in virtue of some other relation's holding between A and Kindness. Similarly,

(10) says that this relation holds between B and Treehood. That is why it would be a mistake to formalize (10) as:

Tree (B, Treehood).

"Tree" cannot reasonably be taken as a relational predicate at all, and is *a fortiori* not the relation signaled by the *pros* in (10). To return to (4), it is because the relation signaled by *pros* is not Unlikeness that (5) and (6) are not equivalent to (4).

Becoming clear about the difference between the two formulations of the conclusion of this argument has thus shown us that the second formulation contains just what we are looking for. That is, we have identified here an occurrence of *pros* in which it introduces a relation unnamed in the sentence. Indeed, we have identified two such occurrences, since it will now be clear that 161c9–d1 (which we have not discussed separately) is just like 161b3–4 in this respect.

What, then, is the relation in question in these sentences? We are clearly in the general area that the Socrates of the first part of the dialogue would associate with forms and participation. But given his demonstrated lack of understanding of those notions, and given that nothing here is explicitly said to be a form, we should not make any rash identifications (e.g., of what I will call "natures" and forms). We must rather let ourselves be guided carefully by the text and then see how to apply its lessons to our views about forms.[7]

If "participation" is not a useful answer now, how can we characterize the relation in question? The answer to this will be of enormous moment in my interpretation of the *Parmenides*. There is nothing particularly controversial about what I will say, but, when combined with the other results of my inquiry, much will develop from it. Let us then look at the information we have, again starting with the first of our two passages.

In order to have some vocabulary to use, but to avoid prejudging any issues by using terms with fixed technical associations, let us say that statements like

Aristides is just

Aristophanes is human

concern the *displays of features by individuals*. Because we wish to deal at this point only with everyday, nontechnical notions, anyone who uses these words for technical purposes should suspend those associations. Thus, "individual" should not be taken as meaning "what cannot be divided further." Also, I am purposely leaving open the question whether features are private to individuals; the everyday notion does not include a fine-grained metaphysical analysis. And this makes it especially useful in connection with Plato, who seems to have wavered on the issue: the *Phaedo* gives prominence to such things as Socrates' Shortness, which other works do not.[8] What will be important for us now is that, whether or not Socrates' features are peculiar to him, his display of them will be a particular display, which is distinct from and may well be different than the displays made by other individuals.

To return now to the *Parmenides*,

The One is unlike the others

and

The others are unlike The One

as used here also concern the features of an individual, The One. (To convince oneself that this is so, it may be helpful to read from the beginning of the fifth hypothesis.)

The additional step made in the interesting, second formulation of the result of our passage involves the introduction of a new term: "Unlikeness" *(anomoiotēs)*. We know that the whole point of using terms in *-otēs* is to make clear that one is referring to abstract qualities rather than to the individual(s) that may exhibit them. (Plato's introduction of the new word *poiotēs* in the *Theaetetus* [at 182a8] makes it a genuinely Platonic word, and "quality" is in a sense the closest translation as having a parallel formation. However, it also has the drawback that our associations with it are heavily influenced if not wholly determined by its narrow use in Aristotle's scheme of categories. In the Platonic sense, Humanity should count as a quality, as do Whiteness, Heat, and Multitude. Because of this, I will be using "property" and "quality" interchangeably.) The notion of properties or qualities in question in the *Parmenides* will be one according to which they are not intrinsically private to individuals. Thus, since I have left open whether features are private, it is also open whether features and properties are identical. If they are not, properties will simply be more general than features.

Our interesting statement says that Unlikeness is that in relation to which the others are unlike The One. So what we are trying to determine is the role a quality has in this kind of case. It is natural to say that the quality is displayed or exhibited, and indeed I have already done so. But the naturalness of the expression can give the feeling that we have a better understanding of the relation in question than we in fact do. We therefore need to consider what Plato might think it amounts to. Uncontroversially, Plato thinks that Unlikeness is what makes things unlike. But we still need to be clearer about the way in which Unlikeness makes things unlike if we are to have any sense of the precise character of the relation it bears to unlike things.

A conservative start is to suppose that the relation in question is some kind of conformability (which, as we have already seen, is a relation that *pros* commonly does indicate). What would be thē point of saying that conformability to Unlikeness bears on The One's being unlike the others? For Plato, how being unlike affects The One is determined by what Unlikeness is. We will therefore understand The One insofar as it is unlike by reference to our understanding of Unlikeness. It may help with this to consider an additional example. Let us return to:

Aristides is just.

Plato would say that Aristides is just in relation to Justice. I suggest that this means that Aristides' display of the feature in question is conformable to Justice (i.e., to what it is to be just). So if Justice is in fact psychic harmony (i.e., being just is having a soul in which each part does its own), Aristides' display of features must conform to that. That is then why he is so unconflicted.

We can now see that the qualities (Justice, Unlikeness, and so on) are playing the roles Plato and others in antiquity assign to natures *(ousiai, phuseis).*[9] So, to sum up (and also to bring in our second passage), we have in each of 161b3–4 and 161c9–d1 an abstract term ("Unlikeness," "Inequality") referring to the nature to which an individual's display of a certain feature is conformable. That is, facts about the nature will in each such case determine (some of) the manifest facts about the individual. And because of this, the nature will be that in light of which we will understand or explain (some of) our observations about the individual, if we do achieve any understanding of them. I believe that Plato intended such cases to fall under the heading of things having predicates in relation to the others.[10] The phrase "in relation to the others" is apposite because the nature named by the abstract term need not be internal to the individual in question, but is in general other than it.[11]

Thus even individuals with no special nature (i.e., the sort of individuals that Plato perhaps believes sensible particulars to be) can have predications in relation to the others true of them. For example, the natures Musicality, Paleness, and so on are all natures to which Socrates' display of features conforms. To invoke natures for this purpose is not yet to make the further and stronger claim that some one nature (say Humanity) is specially Socrates'.

I think the suggestion I have been developing concerning the force of Plato's specification "in relation to the others" fits not only this passage but (as I will undertake to show) the *Parmenides* as a whole. Moreover, as we can note right away, it ties the mysterious device in question to no trivial matters, but to things and relations well known to be central to Platonism.

Predication *Pros Heauto*

We now need to develop a sense of what it is to have a predicate "in relation to oneself." We already are working with a scheme in which natures play an important role. So we can already entertain the possibility that predicates hold of a subject in relation to itself when they are properly connected with the subject's nature. What we now need to find out is what the proper connection is. (What subjects have natures? Notice that, as the previous discussion showed, the circumstance that a nature may be something to which an individual's display of [some] features conforms does not distinguish that nature from the crowd of other natures so related to that individual. Luckily, the gymnastic dialectic presupposes that its subjects are forms, so we are not dealing with subjects like Socrates. We will go on the assumption that each form is specially associated with a nature. Later on, when we are reconstructing our notion of forms, we will determine whether the association is total identity, or something less.)

Since we have already examined all of the occurrences of the preposition *pros* with the accusative in the *Parmenides*, we will now have to be guided by the two tenets mentioned earlier: that all the arguments and their conclusions are to be accepted, and that the first section of arguments is characterized by the *pros heauto* qualification. I shall start from an argument that, when read without qualification, is extremely problematic. I will then be guided in determining the force of the qualification by seeing what qualification, by bearing on it, would make the passage reasonable.

The argument in question appears at 139c3–d1. Its conclusion is typical of the negative results of the first section of arguments constituting the dialectical exercise, and is typically puzzling if read without any qualification. The argument purports to establish that The One cannot be other than anything, as follows:

Ἕτερον δέ γε ἑτέρου οὐκ ἔσται, ἕως ἂν ᾖ ἕν· οὐ γὰρ ἑνὶ προσήκει ἑτέρῳ τινὸς εἶναι, ἀλλὰ μόνῳ ἑτέρῳ ἑτέρου, ἄλλῳ δὲ οὐδενί.—Ὀρθῶς.—Τῷ μὲν ἄρα ἓν εἶναι οὐκ ἔσται ἕτερον· ἢ οἴει;— Οὐ δῆτα.—Ἀλλὰ μὴν εἰ μὴ τούτῳ, οὐχ ἑαυτῷ ἔσται, εἰ δὲ μὴ αὑτῷ, οὐδὲ αὐτό· αὐτὸ δὲ μηδαμῇ ὂν ἕτερον οὐδενὸς ἔσται ἕτερον.—Ὀρθῶς. (139c3–d1)

And it won't be other than another, while it is one. For it's not fitting for The One to be other than something, but only for The Other Than Another, and not for anything else.—Right.—Therefore it won't be other by being one. Or do you think so?—Certainly not.—But if not by this, it won't be by itself, and if not by itself neither ⟨will⟩ it ⟨be other⟩; and it being in no way other will be other than nothing.—Right.

The crucial consideration here is contained in the last two exchanges (139c6–d1). Parmenides seems to make a completely frivolous mistake, wholly irrelevant to the context, at least on an unadorned view of the context (one on which the task of the section is simply to find out what follows for The One, if it is). The argument seems vulnerable to objections like: "You might as well say that the lamp on my desk cannot be yellow, since it is not yellow by being a lamp and if not by itself, neither will *it* be yellow."

This is just the sort of argument that invites rejectionist interpretation. If we look for an interpreter who is trying to uphold the argument, we find Cornford defending it rather gallantly as follows:

The conclusion is sound. To be other than something else is not the same thing as to be one. So a One which is simply one and has no second character at all, cannot have the character of being other than anything. Its "oneness", which is all there is of it, cannot make it so.[12]

We can see the limitations of this defense when we consider taking the analogous line in the lamp case. This would be:

> To be yellow is not the same thing as to be a lamp. So a lamp which is simply a lamp and has no second character at all, cannot have the character of being yellow. Its "lamphood," which is all there is of it, cannot make it so.

This statement immediately invites the suspicion that the inquiry may be horribly misconceived. To introduce an individual with only a single property seems to defy logic: surely there are properties (such as Self-Identity) that every respectable individual must have.[13] This introduction also defies the text: even if we accepted the introduction of a One with no second character as our subject here, this would be a *different* subject from the One that has Being and so on (which will have to be introduced as the subject of the next section). As we have already seen, this leads inappropriately to the multiplication of the hypotheses.

So Cornford's effort to uphold this argument, however gallant, is unconvincing. My original purpose was to find another way of realizing the basic plan (shared with Cornford) of showing the arguments to be good. That purpose has now become more specific: I expect to do this (in the present case) by applying the in-relation-to-itself qualification. We may note right now a grammatical feature of Plato's use of the in-relation-to qualifications that gives hope that they can be applied without generating the problems Cornford did. In the schema:

εἰ ἓν ἔστι / μὴ ἔστι, τί χρὴ συμβαίνειν τῷ ἑνὶ / τοῖς
ἄλλοῖς πρὸς αὑτό / πρὸς τὰ ἄλλα

If The One is / is not, what must follow for The One / for the others
in relation to itself / in relation to the others

the qualifications involving "in relation to" are added not to the antecedent (grammatical protasis) but to the consequent (grammatical apodosis). Since Cornford's difficulties stem from his having to add complications to the antecedents, any advantages that can be obtained by the use of the treatment of these qualifications can be obtained without those difficulties.

Let us return to the step in the argument that needs explanation. It was:

Τῷ μὲν ἄρα ἓν εἶναι οὐκ ἔσται ἕτερον . . . εἰ δὲ μὴ αὑτῷ, οὐδὲ αὐτό· (139c6–8)

Therefore, it won't be other by being one . . . and if not by itself, neither will *it* be other.

Now, given our attention to the qualifications, we see the conclusion here as being implicitly:

οὐδὲ αὐτὸ ⟨πρὸς αὑτό⟩

neither will *it* be other ⟨in relation to itself⟩.

We are going to work from three salient points about this passage:

    (a) the appearance of the phrase *toī hen einai* (by being one)
    (b) the appearance of the phrase *heautōi* (by itself)
    (c) the circumstance that we think the result should be characterized as *pros heauto*.

Together with the progress we have made in understanding Plato's in-relation-to qualifications, (c) suggests that the passage should concern itself with predicates that hold of the One in virtue of having the proper connection with The One's nature. (We have not yet determined what the proper connection is.)

This expectation is encouraged by (b): the passage speaks of what The One is *by itself*. This clearly is trying to get at something very special or internal to The One; there is an implicit contrast to other things that The One is, but not by itself. A role for natures in specifying what makes some things true of The One *by itself* would not be surprising. And indeed the passage is easy to construe as giving such a role to natures, given (a): the appearance of *toī hen einai* ("by being one"). For the passage makes the move from not being other by being one to not being other by itself. And *to hen einai* is obviously an expression one could use to name The One's nature.

Once we take this hint, it turns out that the following three formulations are all equivalent:

Being X is part of being one.

The nature of X is part of the nature of The One.

The nature X-hood is part of the nature Unity.

Let us now return to the argument of our passage. It no longer looks mistaken or frivolous. For we can now go beyond the statement with which we started that predicates will hold of The One in relation to itself when they have the proper connection with The One's nature. We can suppose that The One is X in relation to itself when being X is a part of being one. (That is, when the nature of X is part of the nature of The One, or put in the third possible way, when X-hood is part of Unity. Because this requirement in terms of a relation between natures makes a demonstration that The One is not X by being one a demonstration that it is not X in relation to itself, the argument of our passage can now be seen to do its job in the most straightforward way.

I would like to turn next to 139d1–e4, the passage immediately following the present one, so as to get more support for the partial characterization we have reached of this section. To be sure of the details of this argument and the interpretation of each step will require lengthy discussion to which I will return later. However we may note that a crucial role is played by the claim:

Οὐχ ἥπερ τοῦ ἑνὸς φύσις, αὐτὴ δήπου καὶ τοῦ ταὐτοῦ. (139d2–3)

That which is the nature of The One is surely not the nature of The Same.

The prominence enjoyed here by a claim concerning relations between natures confirms the idea we have been developing that determining such connections is central to the purpose of this section. For the passage I first discussed used such phrases as

by being one

in such a way that I connected it with speculations involving an appeal to natures. That connection is strengthened by a claim about relations between natures and actual use of the word *phusis* in the very next argument.

Suggestive passages have now provided us with an idea of what inquiry concerning something *pros heauto* is: it is grounded in relations between natures. I would like, finally, to complete our notion of predication *pros heauto*, so that we will be in a position to go through the dialogue and see how the notion does its work there.

Let us consider the sort of genus-species tree familiar to us from, for example, the Linnaean classification system. To illustrate the idea, we

might imagine a tree showing the Animals. We can imagine dividing
Animal into Vertebrate and Invertebrate, dividing Vertebrate in turn
into Mammal and so on, and continuing with such divisions through
Feline and Cat, to produce at last such *infimae species* as Persian Cat.[14]
In the *Sophist, Statesman,* and *Philebus* Plato devotes a great deal of
attention to such trees, discussing explicitly the methodology of con-
structing them, as well as providing numerous examples. In such a
tree, a kind A appears either directly below or far below another kind
B if what it is to be an A is to be a B with a certain differentia (or
series of differentiae) added.[15] That is, the natures of A's and B's are
so related that being a B is part of what it is to be an A.

We may formulate precisely our notion of predication *pros heauto*
by saying that in any such case B can be truly predicated of A (or of
The A) *pros heauto,* and so can A, and so can any of the differentiae
D. The idea here is that this kind of predication is grounded in the
structure of the nature in question: A's nature is what it is to be (an)
A—that is, (a) B with . . . with D, and it is in virtue of this that the
predications hold.

It may be helpful at this point to take some examples of true predications *pros heauto*. We will get sentences like:

The Just is virtuous.

Dancing moves.[16]

Humanity is rational.

The Just is just.

It is clear that such sentences come out true in Plato's work, as well
as fitting our characterization of the *pros heauto*.

The Just is virtuous

holds because of the relationship between the natures associated with
its subject and predicate terms; being virtuous is part of what it is to
be just. Or we can describe the predication as holding because Justice
is a kind of Virtue. We can also see that

Dancing moves

is a true predication *pros heauto,* since Motion figures in the account
of what Dancing is. If we for the moment pay ourselves the compli-

ment of supposing that we are correctly classified as a rational kind of Animal (i.e., that our *differentia* is Rational), then

Humanity is rational

holds too. Finally,

The Just is just

turns out to exemplify the limit case of predication *pros heauto:* it is uninformative but safe. Thus ''self-predication'' sentences can be used to make true predications *pros heauto,* though not all predications *pros heauto* are of the form: The A is A. (Sometimes in what follows, when reminding readers of how predications *pros heauto* function, I will speak of the predicates' being elements in the correct accounts of the subjects' natures, of one nature's being a part of another, and so on. I of course do not mean to exclude the limit case in which the natures are identical, but it seems too cumbersome always to be mentioning it. All such statements should be understood in light of the present, fuller explication.)

We should remark at this point how this specification of which predications are true *pros heauto* differs from one on which only those of the form

The A is A

would count. Either way of delimiting the class seems compatible with the phrase *pros heauto.* However, I choose the wider class because the circumstance that in general there are more *pros heauto* predications possible than just the trivial one makes inquiring into which such predications hold interesting in a way in which it would otherwise not be: it would be ludicrous to consider any other sentence than the obvious ''self-predication'' sentence if one knew in advance that it was going to be the only *pros heauto* truth. (Nor would amassing such sentences be very informative.) On the wider view, however, there is a point to asking whether A is X *pros heauto.* Where A and X are not identical, this is equivalent to asking whether X appears above A in A's tree. This would have to be answered separately for each X, by getting out the accounts of X and of A and by working out the relevant portions of trees.

Inquiry of this kind is familiar to us from earlier works as part of the Platonist program (it makes its appearance as early as the *Euthy-*

phro, at 11e ff., and seems to be relevant to the famous passage at *Phaedo* 103 ff.), as well as playing a prominent role in the later works in the form of collection and division of genera and species. Because this understanding of inquiry into what results for things in relation to themselves is tied to a project of long-standing importance to Plato, it promises to sustain the burden of showing why he gave the qualification a central role in generating sections of gymnastic dialectic. Thus, both of the in-relation-to qualifications have now been understood as useful linguistic instruments for their author.

Summary of Our Understanding of the Qualifications

We may now sum up our present understanding of the in-relation-to qualifications as follows. The qualifications belong to the kind of use of the preposition *pros* in which a sentence of the form

A is B *pros* C

A is B in relation to C

indicates that some relation unnamed in the sentence is relevant to A's being B. In the *Parmenides,* the qualifications mark a difference in *the way in which* B can be predicated of A. They do this by indicating the relations that ground each of the two kinds of predication. Thus, the difference between what holds of a subject in relation to itself and what holds of the same subject in relation to the others is not simply due to the distinction between the others and the subject. It derives more fundamentally from the fact that a different relation is involved in each kind of case. Predications of a subject *pros heauto* hold in virtue of a relation internal to the subject's own nature. Predications *pros ta alla* on the other hand concern individuals' displays of features, which Plato takes to involve a relation to natures—that is, to other things.

We can now observe that the *pros heauto* truth

The Just is virtuous

is not concerned with the same kind of fact as the *pros ta alla* assertion

Aristides is virtuous.

The *pros heauto* truth holds because Justice is a kind of Virtue. It offers an analysis of the nature in question. The *pros ta alla* assertion, on the other hand, does not analyze any nature. Rather, it informs us about a region of the world where the nature is exhibited; in our example, it concerns the display of features by the individual, Aristides. The basic difference then between such predications *pros ta alla* (which we in the twentieth century think of as common or garden predications) and predications *pros heauto* is that predications *pros heauto* are not concerned with saying that individuals exhibit features. They have a role Plato regarded as more fundamental—namely, one of presenting the internal structures of the real natures.

Finally, let us observe that the distinction in question is not a way of subdividing the class of predications we ourselves are in the habit of making, as the distinction between essential and accidental predication can be. That is, the essential/accidental distinction can be wielded within a collection of sentences we commonly assent to so as to separate:

Callias is human

on the one hand, from

Callias is pale

on the other. In terms of the distinction introduced in the *Parmenides,* however, both of these sample sentences are predications *pros ta alla:* they both concern the display of features by the individual, Callias.[17] Predications *pros heauto* on the other hand have an altogether different (and in Plato's view more fundamental) use; they hold in virtue of reflecting genus-species structures (which they do by showing the internal structures of properties). Thus

Humanity has vertebrae

is a true predication *pros heauto* not in virtue of the fact that some abstract entity comes equipped with a backbone (there is no such fact) but because being vertebrate is part of what it is to be a human being.

Categorizing Sentences

There is a general fact about our two kinds of predication that will be
of considerable importance in interpreting the totality of the arguments
forming the gymnastic dialectic (the task of the chapters to come). So
I would like to get clear about the general fact now. It will emerge
most clearly, I think, by contrast: we can start by considering a familiar feature of certain other distinctions and then come to see that thinking of the *pros heauto/pros ta alla* distinction in the same way is a
mistake.

Let us start by observing that distinctions such as the necessary/
contingent distinction and the analytic/synthetic distinction are understood in such a way as to make these classifications exclusive. For
example, it being necessary that nine is odd, there is no room for a
contingent truth that nine is odd, still less for a contingent truth that
nine is not odd. Similarly when the contingent truth that the cat is on
the mat holds, there is no necessary truth that that cat is on the mat,
let alone a necessary truth that it is not. It is clear that the analytic/
synthetic distinction, if it could be drawn successfully, would have
this same exclusive character.

The essential/accidental distinction displays a similar feature. That
is, it is generally deployed within a framework within which every
subject-predicate sentence can be classified as making either an essential or an accidental predication, and not both. A further point about
the essential/accidental distinction is of some interest. If we accept a
certain kind of metaphysics, it can turn out that some properties are
had essentially or not at all, whereas others are always accidents. The
additional tenet here might be expressed by saying that substance (or
natural kind) terms are predicated essentially, and all others acciden-
tally. Thus someone who accepts the additional tenet can end by concluding that a person who knows which are the substance (or natural
kind) terms can tell just by inspection whether a given sentence makes
an essential or an accidental predication, depending on which type the
predicate term is suited for. For example,

Our cat is sleepy

can be seen right away to predicate an accident, while

Our cat is an animal

would clearly attribute an essential property to the object in question.

Let us now turn to the *pros heauto/pros ta alla* distinction, and ask ourselves whether such sentences as

(1) The One is not many

(2) The One does not have parts

are such as to be classified as definitely *pros heauto* or again as definitely *pros ta alla*.

Keeping in mind the specifications we have reached of these two kinds of predication, we can see that along the lines of

The Just is just *(pros heauto)*

The Just is virtuous *(pros heauto)*

we might also get

The Many is many *(pros heauto)*

The Composite has parts *(pros heauto)*.

Of course it is natural to expect that negative statements involving this type of predication should be possible—for example,

(3) The Triangle is not just *(pros heauto)*

(4) The Cat is not the same *(pros heauto)*.

These would have the force: Triangularity does not stand in the specified relation to Justice, nor does Cathood to Sameness. Both assertions are true, since being just is not involved in being a triangle, nor is Sameness part of Cathood.

Now notice that The Cat can perfectly well be said to be the same, where this is not understood as a claim *pros heauto*. For

The Cat is the same *(pros ta alla)*

claims that The Cat displays a certain feature, not—what (4) denies—that Cat is a species of Same. Again, since The Cat is not the same (sc., as something else), Plato would consider it correct to say

The Cat is not the same *(pros ta alla)*

and this would have a different force from the force of (4).

We can now see that

(a) The One is not many *(pros heauto)*

and

(b) The One is not many *(pros ta alla)*

are both viable assertions (indeed, both are true as we will learn by studying the *Parmenides*). However, (a) and (b) are not interchangeable: (a) asserts that being many is not part of what it is to be one; (b) that a certain individual, The One, is not a plurality. We might compare

Green is not a color

and

Green is not a colored thing

which very obviously do not have the same truth value and so are clearly not interchangeable. Since neither (a) nor (b) has a claim to be what

(1) The One is not many

is always aiming at, we cannot take one of them as the full expression of (1) and read off from it the appropriate character. This leaves us to realize that certain sentences, of which (1) and (2) are representative, can be asserted in virtue of either of a pair whose members are one from each of our two classes of predications.

Conclusion

We have established that the in-relation-to qualifications do pertain to the second part of the dialogue, and determined the force of each. They mark a distinction between two kinds of predication—that is, they introduce a difference in the way in which one term may be predicated of another. "In relation to itself" signals that the predication reveals the structure of the subject's own nature. "In relation to the others," on the other hand, marks predications that concern their subjects' display of some feature conformably to something other—namely, the nature associated with that feature. We also found that given a form of words

A is B

one cannot tell immediately whether to take it as a claim *pros heauto* or as a claim *pros ta alla*. The fact that it can be used in each way will be of great importance for the interpretation of the *Parmenides*, ultimately enabling us to face the systematic grammatical contradictions between the conclusions of various sections without worry.

A final remark should be made about the *pros heauto/pros ta alla* distinction. It can now be seen to coincide with the distinction between the *kath' hauto* and *pros allo* uses of ''is'' in the *Sophist*.[18] Thus, not only are the notions invoked in describing the force of the distinction connected with concerns of Plato's, but the very distinction itself is drawn in two of the late dialogues. This is added confirmation for my identification, since it is desirable to recognize continuity in Plato's work.[19]

4

The Exercise Interpreted: The First Section

Parmenides' labored description of required sections of argument originally held out little hope of guidance in interpreting the second part of the dialogue. This was because the description, though careful and detailed, seemed to be unintelligible: it employed in a crucial role a pair of qualifications to whose meaning we had no clue. However, by considering these phrases in connection with selected passages from the second part of the dialogue, we have succeeded in interpreting the in-relation-to qualifications. We know now that to derive results for something in relation to itself is to determine what appears above it in a correct genus-species tree—that is, to determine what natures are parts of its nature. Investigation of something in relation to the others involves a quite different kind of inquiry, determining what features the individual in question exhibits. With these in-relation-to qualifications interpreted, the list of section descriptions produced in chapter 2 becomes quite informative, and so the claim that it fits the second part of the dialogue can be tested. We now need to find out whether the actual sections of argument that Parmenides produces there in fact match these descriptions.

In this and the following four chapters, I will show that they do. To achieve this, I will indicate how I construe each of the arguments appearing in the second part of the *Parmenides*. (I will not discuss every argument individually, but I will discuss enough representative ones so that my discussion will make clear how I construe the passages not treated explicitly.) I will also in many cases discuss other ways of construing the arguments. This will suggest, I think, that the interpretation my framework yields is not merely compatible with the text; it is also the most successful of the various ways of explaining these passages. In the present chapter, I will interpret the first section of arguments forming Parmenides' dialectical display. I will then continue, in the chapters that follow, to take up the arguments in the order in which they appear in the dialogue.

Before considering the arguments, however, it may be helpful to discuss some general observations about the section, which amounts to noting problems that the section has appeared to present. First of all, the conclusions of this section seem to be in systematic contradiction with those of the second section. Apparent systematic contradiction with the results of another section is, of course, characteristic of all the sections of Parmenides' exercise. But the first pair of sections forces us, for the first time, to come to terms with the issue. That is, if we are unwilling to accept contradiction, we are faced with a choice between interpreting the results so that they are not in contradiction after all, or rejecting half of the results Parmenides claims to establish (in such a way as to remove one member from each contradictory pair).

Next, even when this first section is taken by itself, its results seem unacceptable. The section purports to demonstrate among other things that, if The One is, The One is not the same as itself, nor is it other than anything, nor does it have Being. In fact, all of the candidate predicates that are canvassed in this section are denied to The One. Thus, if we read these results as "ordinary" predications, this section claims that, if The One is, it lacks various features that it seems *anything* would have to possess.

Finally, if we read the conclusions of each of these arguments as denying that a certain individual, The One, lacks some feature, then many of the arguments for these conclusions are problematic. That is, the arguments Parmenides gives cannot be construed so as to succeed in establishing that The One lacks all of these features. Thus, if that is their purpose, many of the arguments are bad.

In the face of these problems, two main kinds of interpretation have been developed. One deals with all three problems at once by a commitment to reject the conclusions of this section. But this type of interpretation is not acceptable (see chapter 1). The other type, more acceptable but with some drawbacks, introduces a subject for this section that is distinct from that of the next one, so removing worry about contradiction between sections.

The Neoplatonist tradition, which notoriously follows this multiple-subject strategy, takes the denial that the subject of the first hypothesis exhibits features such as Being and Self-Identity as showing just how unusual and special this subject is. That is, this tradition boldly embraces the second problem as if it were unproblematic. Cornford—while he agrees with the Neoplatonists that the section shows that if its special subject is, then it lacks all the features in question—departs from their example (and so produces what I called in chapter 1 a "mixed interpretation") in finding such an entity to be impossible and rejecting the postulation of this subject. He thus manages to escape the second problem. But Cornford, precisely because he takes the unacceptability of the description of the subject that emerges from the conclusions of the section to be motivation to reject the hypothesis from which those conclusions are derived, is committed to the validity of the arguments that derive those conclusions from the hypothesis. Thus he has serious difficulties in the area of the third problem. As we will see, his effort to portray the section as arguing well for the conclusions as he reads them is unsuccessful. The Neoplatonists, whose understanding of the conclusions is similar to that of Cornford (and who differ from him most obviously in not rejecting the results), also face the difficulty that attaches to any attempt to make the arguments respectable, on this reading of the conclusions. That is, even if one is willing to embrace an entity lacking all the features in question, there is still the problem of why Plato gave inadequate arguments to prove his results about this unusual subject.

We are now in a position to understand this section in an entirely novel way. For (as acute readers may already have noticed) the apparent problems of this section and the interpretations that responded to them all share a certain reading of the conclusions: as denying that a certain individual has each of a series of features—that is, as making what we have come to call predications *pros ta alla*. Our investigations, however, cause us to think (end of chapter 3) that these sentences *can be used in another way* (to make predications *pros heauto*) and also (chapter 2) that the results of this section indeed *will be* of this latter type.

We can already appreciate the difference our expectation, if realized, will make to the problems. If, as we expect, the results of this section are to be taken as predications *pros heauto,* whereas those of the second section are predications *pros ta alla,* the grammatical contradictions between the sections will be no source of worry. There is no real tension between, for example, the claim that The One is not other *pros heauto,* and the claim that The One *is* other *pros ta alla.* The first is true in virtue of the fact that being other is not part of what it is to be one, whereas the second holds since the individual, The One, is indeed other than some things. So our framework has the resources to make the problem of the contradictions between sections dissolve.

The next problem concerned the peculiarity of an entity lacking features that any respectable entity would seem to require. This problem clearly depends on reading the results of the section as predications *pros ta alla.* As predications *pros heauto,* they do not deny features to an individual; they rather deny that a certain kind appears below certain other kinds in a genus-species tree. There is nothing paradoxical about saying, "One is not a species of Other, that is, being other is not part of what it is to be one," as there is about saying, "The One is not other than anything."

The final problem involved the adequacy of the arguments to support their results. To see whether they can establish the results read as predications *pros heauto,* we will have to look at the individual arguments. But the *pros heauto* reading of the conclusions is different enough from the standard reading to make the circumstance that the arguments formerly looked bad no indication that they will continue to do so. If our interpretation is the first to be able to show the arguments really are good ones,[1] that will be a strong point in its favor.

We have already noted, in the case of the one argument from the section we have discussed (in chapter 3), the unsatisfactory ring that is characteristic of this section, as customarily read. In that case, we showed the argument to be sound by sympathetic understanding of its conclusion as a predication *pros heauto.* In what follows, I claim that the remaining arguments of the section are also best construed in accordance with this understanding. Thus, the expectations we formed on the basis of our interpretation of the methodological remarks are realized in this case.

The section is indeed organized as a response to what we could call the "theme question": If The One is, what follows for The One in relation to itself? The purpose of the section is to determine what appears above One is a correct genus-species tree—that is, what appears in the account telling what it is to be one. When the conclusions of the section are construed as predications *pros heauto,* they are un-surprisingly true: The One is a species of none of the kinds considered here. On this reading of the conclusions, there will no longer appear to be any bad arguments in the section.

There will, however, be some variety in the way in which the particular results are established. There will be two very different types of "starting point" from which Parmenides will develop arguments in this section. One will be just *seeing* (in certain cases) that a certain kind cannot appear above The One. A kind's being excluded in this way from The One's tree can then provide material for arguments ruling out further predications *pros heauto.* The other type of starting point will be the observed pattern of the displays of features by particulars. Although such facts are not about relations between natures in the first instance (I hope so much is clear, after chapter 3), it will be seen that they can have *implications* in that domain. Let us now turn to the text.

The hypothesis for the section is: If The One is. Its first result is: The One will not be many. Because Parmenides derives a series of other results using arguments that will take this one as their starting point, we need to determine not just what the force of this first result is and why we should accept it, but also how it can be used to obtain further results. I will take up each of these two tasks in turn.

What the text has to say in presenting this result is confined to:

εἰ ἕν ἐστιν, ἄλλο τι οὐκ ἂν εἴη πολλὰ τὸ ἕν;—Πῶς γὰρ ἄν;

If The One is, The One wouldn't be many?—How would it be?

Let us start by considering ways of taking the result as a predication *pros ta alla,* and interpretations that provide explanations as to why Parmenides and Aristotle (the interlocutor) accept the result so interpreted. (This type of interpretation is of course not the type I will accept; but it seems only fair to consider whether it may not be viable.)

On Cornford's view,[2] this sentence, though it appears to state something that *follows from* the hypothesis (If The One is), is really to be understood as the *expression of the definition* of the subject of the section (a One that is simply one and has no second character).[3] Cornford explains the form of expression by saying that Plato seeks to follow the model of the historical Parmenides.[4] This solution is of marginal elegance. Given the grammatical form of the sentence in question as a conditional, with

The One will not be many

the *consequent* (grammatical apodosis), it is undesirable to take it as a covertly introduced premise that The One is not many. Also, this explanation seems to deprive the pages of argument that form the rest of the section of any useful purpose: if the subject is defined as having no second character, why argue to rule out any particular ones?[5]

So, we would like to find an interpretation of

The One is not many

according to which it could follow from

The One is.

If the conclusion is to be a *pros ta alla* claim, two possible ways of making the transition suggest themselves. They are:

(I) If The One is, The One is one *(pros ta alla)*.
Nothing can be one *(pros ta alla)* and also be many *(pros ta alla)*.
The One is not many *(pros ta alla)*.

(II) If The One is, The One is one *(pros ta alla)*.
The One has a special way of being one *(pros ta alla)* that excludes being many *(pros ta alla)*.
The One is not many *(pros ta alla)*.

(I) is not convincing because it relies on a premise that is not only false but to which the dialogue has drawn attention as being false. At 129c4–d6, in his exchange with Zeno, Socrates pointed out that there is nothing problematic in an individual's being one and many—for example, one person and many limbs. It is therefore not to be supposed that Plato here blithely expects that *nothing* can be both one and many. (II) suggests itself as an improvement on (I) but does not by itself tell us what this special way of being one is and how it manages to exclude being many. The weakness of the passage when interpreted along these lines joins with the expectation based on our reading of the transitional methodological remarks and suggests that we not take the result in question as a *pros ta alla* claim.

The suggestion is confirmed when we consider how easy it is to see the truth of:

> The One is not many *pros heauto*.

If The One were going to be many *pros heauto,* Many would have to appear above One in a correct tree, or else occupy the same position in virtue of being identical with One. Obviously Many and One are not identical. Nor are they related in such a way as to make Many properly appear above One: being one is not a kind or way of being many. So much must be obvious to anyone who knows that one and many are opposites (i.e., to virtually everyone). This obvious thing is what is expressed by the *pros heauto* claim: The One is not many.

The self-evidence of the result on this reading is actually a point in favor of the reading: an interpretation that posits a nonobvious argument has to explain why the argument does not appear in the text, which was quoted earlier.

Now that we have a satisfactory reading of this first result, we are ready to go on to our second task: explaining how it leads to the others that depend explicitly on it. For in my view, this first result is a "starting point." That is, we see that it holds without argument (though there is a reason for accepting it, based on our understanding of one and many as opposites). And the result, once obtained, will then be used in generating further results by means of arguments. We are now ready to determine how this result can be used to derive others.

The key point to realize here is that, because of the structures of the trees that lie behind them, predications *pros heauto* are transitive. For example, since Cat is quadruped and Quadruped is animal, Cat is animal *(pros heauto)*.[6] And in general, if we have

> S is R *pros heauto*

this is because S *is* (R with XYZ). So if it also turns out that R itself has as its full account (ABC with Q), then we can specify S more explicitly as (ABC with Q with XYZ). This makes evident that Q is also a *pros heauto* predicate of S. Thus, the following principle holds:

If Q is predicated *pros heauto* of R, and R is in turn predicated *pros heauto* of S, then Q is a *pros heauto* predicate of S.

From this we can derive also:

If Q is predicated *pros heauto* of R, but not of S, then R cannot itself be predicated *pros heauto* of S.

For if R were predicated *pros heauto* of S, then, by our initial principle, since Q is predicated *pros heauto* of R, Q would also have to be predicated *pros heauto* of S, but we are here supposing precisely that Q is not predicated *pros heauto* of S.

This second principle gives point to the project of connecting candidate predicates with being many: anything that involves being many *pros heauto* cannot be predicated of The One *pros heauto* (now that it has been established that many cannot itself be so predicated). I understand the arguments from 137c5–138b6 as carrying out this project. Parmenides there rules out as *pros heauto* predicates of The One: having parts, being a whole, having beginning, middle, or end, having limit, having shape (being curved or straight), and being anywhere (in itself or another). All these are analyzed so as to involve being many. Thus, although the result that The One is not many is not itself derived by argument, it serves a key role as a starting point for arguments Parmenides does give.

To help readers to compare my interpretation with the family that would not give a *pros heauto* reading to these conclusions, it may be useful to note here that on the conventional reading of the first result (that The One is not many), a transitivity principle would of course also be available, so that family of readings can also explain the derivation of the additional results *given the first one*. But this does not remove the paradoxical air the results have when read as denying that The One exhibits these features. This is, I think, due to the fact that, although the additional results may follow given the first one, the first one itself as conventionally understood (no matter what interpreters may say) is in fact false.

Parmenides next considers whether The One can be in motion or at rest. He rules out motion indirectly: being in motion is said to take the form of either locomotion or alteration. He then rules out that The One has locomotion or alteration as a predicate. As we will see, the argument supposes that this automatically excludes the more general predicate. The argument opens by excluding alteration.

Ὅρα δή, οὕτως ἔχον εἰ οἷόν τέ ἐστιν ἑστάναι ἢ κινεῖσθαι.—Τί δὴ γὰρ οὔ;—Ὅτι κινούμενόν γε ἢ φέροιτο ἢ ἀλλοιοῖτο ἄν· αὗται γὰρ μόναι κινήσεις.—Ναί.—Ἀλλοιούμενον δὲ τὸ ἓν ἑαυτοῦ ἀδύνατόν που ἓν ἔτι εἶναι.—Ἀδύνατον.—Οὐκ ἄρα κατ᾽ ἀλλοίωσίν γε κινεῖται.—Οὐ φαίνεται. (138b7–c4)

Cornford renders this as follows:

> Next consider whether, such being its condition, it can be in motion or at rest. If it were in motion, it would have to be either moving in place or undergoing alteration; for there are no other kinds of motion. Now, if the One alters, so as to become different from itself, it surely cannot still be one. Therefore, it does not move in the sense of suffering alteration.

He then explains this by writing:

> The word for change or alteration *(alloiōsis)*, as distinct from local motion, is used in its widest sense, covering any properties which might be altered so that the thing should become "other" than it was. . . . But here the only possible change is that the One (which has no second property that it could lose by alteration) should cease to be one. But this would mean its complete disappearance, not alteration; and even disappearance is impossible: the One cannot cease to exist, since (as we shall discover later, 141e) it has not the second property, existence.[7]

We may say that Cornford clearly takes

The One does not alter

as having *pros ta alla* force. He then thinks the passage argues well for that conclusion, using the covert definition of the subject as a premise. However, since we do not wish to subscribe to his scheme of introducing covert definitions of distinct subjects, we may of course not accept this explanation.

It would clearly be possible to take the passage as giving the very argument Cornford provided, without his supplementary premise, but then the argument seems to need some other supplement. For the argument without supplement would be something like:

If The One changes, it changes from being one *(pros ta alla)*

So it cannot change and still display Unity as a feature.

The assumption that any change involves a change from being one is going to seem illicit unless it could receive some support showing that the only feature that The One has is its Unity. Conceivably this could be supplied, but, since this argument occurs when many features have still to be excluded (even on an interpretation according to which the arguments that have appeared before this one have been excluding features that The One might have had), it would be premature to rely on this now.

We have been looking at ways of taking this claim, when it is read as a predication *pros ta alla*. That is, we have been looking at a family of interpretations different from the one we expect to adopt: we expect that the result is in fact a predication *pros heauto*. If we start again from the opening of the passage, we can see how well it lends itself to an approach in terms of *pros heauto* predications. For we can take the second of Parmenides' sentences as inking in a bit of a tree. It ran:

Ὅτι κινούμενόν γε ἢ φέροιτο ἢ ἀλλοιοῖτο ἄν· αὗται γὰρ μόναι κινήσεις. (138b8–c1)

This is as much as to say: the genus Motion has exactly two species, Locomotion and Alteration.

Now it remains to see whether what follows makes sense if we take this view of the opening. The crux is going to be the exclusion of alteration. Here, as in the case of the exclusion of many (the first result of this section of arguments), I believe that Cornford has gone wrong by trying to provide an argument where Plato intended none. (Of course, in each case, the result *on Cornford's reading* is counter-intuitive enough to require justification. This is just an indication that some other reading, on which the result would not call out for defense, is preferable.) After all, the exclusion of alteration consists solely in the remark:

Ἀλλοιούμενον δὲ τὸ ἓν ἑαυτοῦ ἀδύνατόν που ἓν ἔτι εἶναι. (138c1–2)

Cornford's interpretation lies behind his translation of this passage:

> Now, if the One alters, so as to become different from itself, it surely cannot still be one.

But there is another way of taking the sentence: to read it as saying that, being altered *(pros heauto)*, it would not be possible for The One still to be one *(pros heauto)*. Since this is not especially counterintuitive, Parmenides could be just stating this fact and relying on its being clear to anyone who thinks about it. This then would be a "starting point," similar to that which we found in the first result of the section. That is, Parmenides would be relying on us just to *see* that it is impossible that Altered should appear above One in a correct tree: anything that was a species of Altered could not be the kind under investigation, One. This result will then be used in further argumentation. For Locomotion will be excluded in its turn by the old strategy of showing that it involves something that has already been excluded: having parts. And then, with both of its species (Locomotion and Alteration) eliminated, it will be seen that Motion cannot appear above One. It could not do so without Locomotion or Alteration appearing above One, or being identical with One (since Motion's species have to appear directly below it, and we know that these are its *only* species). That is, it could not do so without The One having as a predicate *pros heauto* something we know it does not have.[8]

Parmenides' demonstration that The One is not at rest needs no separate attention. As usual, its initially bizarre air is dispelled when we take it as a predication *pros heauto*. (There is no violation of the wished-for tranquillity of the forms in saying that being at rest is not part of what it is to be one.) We find here a now-familiar argument pattern. Parmenides eliminates the candidate predicate by showing a connection between it and another that has already been excluded.

The next passage to be discussed is 139d1 ff. We have already met a part of it: this confirmed the conjecture I developed in chapter 3 that natures play an important role in prediction *pros heauto*. In that connection, I quoted only the statement:

Οὐχ ἥπερ τοῦ ἑνὸς φύσις, αὐτὴ δήπου καὶ τοῦ ταὐτοῦ. (139d2–3)

That which is the nature of The One is surely not the nature of The Same.

I then remarked on its being well adapted to play a role in an inquiry of the type I identified in 139c3–d1. That is, its dealing in connections between natures seemed to suit it to be used in inquiry into what predicates The One has *pros heauto,* as I was beginning to understand such inquiry. I did not then discuss the lines that support this statement of Parmenides.

We now need to look at these, and also consider the context in which this assertion has its role. For one thing, we need to make sure that the argument given to support this statement gives it the force required for the role for which I said it was adapted, and that this is indeed the role it plays in its actual context. Also, the last result of this passage, that The One is not the same as itself, initially seems rather bizarre, and so is adapted to serve as a test case for interpretative schemes. In fact, the result will not be at all bizarre on my reading of it. Moreover, examination of this passage will lead us to recognize Parmenides' use of a new kind of starting point for arguments—namely, observation of the pattern of features displayed by particulars.

Since there is a rather bewildering variety of ways of taking several of the crucial steps in the argument we have here, it will be convenient to start with the larger picture of the strategy of the passage and the outline of the argument in question, as I understand them. The overall purpose of the passage is to show that The One is not the same, and so not the same as itself. By this point in our investigations, it should need no more than a brief indication to draw attention to the fantastic quality these assertions have, it read as "ordinary" predications. But there is yet hope that as a predication *pros heauto,*

The One is not the same

may be true. This would then lead by application of the transitivity principles to the further *pros heauto* conclusion:

The One is not the same as itself.

Our expectation is, of course, that this is the way to understand these statements.

But notice that here, the result

The One is not the same

from which the final result

The One is not the same as itself

will be easily derived, is not obviously true, even when we tell ourselves to try understanding it as a predication *pros heauto*. Whereas
there was something immediately acceptable about, for example, the
claim that being many has nothing to do with what it is to be one, a
similar claim about being one and being the same does not have that
kind of *immediate* credibility. I mention this not just because it is true,
but rather because reflection on it bears both on the strategy of the
passage, and also on the way in which I think our argument will obtain
its "starting point."

It seems to me that the reason we are not willing immediately to
repudiate the suggestion that maybe The One is the same *pros heauto*
is that we think perhaps for things to be the same *just is* for them to
be one with each other (and also that for things to be one just is for
them to be the same as each other). This suggests that maybe the
natures of The One and The Same are identical, so that the *pros heauto*
predication of either of the other would hold. However, the thought
that One is *just one species* of Same has much less plausibility. (In
this case, one way of things being the same would be to be one, but
there would also be other ways.) One way of making the implausibility of the thought more apparent is to try to think what the other species would be. That is, entertain the possibility of supposing that the
species of Same are One and Many; or that they are One and Cat. So
if any *pros heauto* predication of Same of The One is going to hold,
it seems most likely to be in virtue of their identity.

I suggest that this is the reason that Parmenides only offers an argument against this identity. The other putative trees that could support the *pros heauto* predication of Same of The One are so implausible that they can be dropped tacitly. The interesting claim that needs
to be disposed of is the claim that The Same and The One have the
identical nature in common. Parmenides (and Aristotle) are willing to
suppose that when they have shown that the natures of The Same and
The One are not identical, they will have done enough to establish that
The One is not the same *pros heauto*. This is the point about the
strategy of the passage that I said would emerge.

But I said that something else would emerge, and this concerns the
"starting point" for our argument. We find ourselves in a position in
which it is not immediately obvious to us that a certain pair of natures
does not really coincide. How can we prove that these natures do not?
I claim that Parmenides here uses observation of the pattern of features

that particulars exhibit to derive an implication for the relevant natures. Here, for the first time in the dialectic, we have an argument that will employ considerations not in the first instance about connections between natures.

We can immediately see that it is not acceptable to give identity conditions for natures by saying:

> Whenever natures have in common all particulars that exhibit them, the natures are the same.

However, it is also clear that the other direction

> When natures are the same they must have in common all particulars that exhibit them

must hold. Therefore, a putative identity between natures can be defeated by producing counterexamples—that is, cases in which one nature is exhibited and the other is not. In fact, the heart of this passage is the subargument to defeat the putative identity between The One and The Same, which proceeds precisely by indicating such a group of counterexamples. I will give the text of the subargument now, and complete my discussion of how it fits into the larger passage. Then I will return to make plausible the subargument's crucial claim about the availability of counterexamples.

The text (at 139d3–e1) of the subargument runs as follows:

(1) Ὅτι οὐκ, ἐπειδὰν ταὐτὸν γένηταί τῷ τι, ἓν γίγνεται. (139d3–4)

(2) Τοῖς πολλοῖς ταὐτὸν γενόμενον πολλὰ ἀνάγκη γίγνεσθαι ἀλλ' οὐχ ἕν. (139d4–5)

(3) Ἀλλ' εἰ τὸ ἓν καὶ τὸ ταὐτὸν μηδαμῇ διαφέρει, ὁπότε τι ταὐτὸν ἐγίγνετο, ἀεὶ ἂν ἓν ἐγίγνετο, καὶ ὁπότε ἕν, ταὐτόν. (139d6–e1)

(1) For it is not the case, whenever something becomes the same as something, that it becomes one.

(2) Becoming the same with many, it must become many, not one.

(3) But if The One and The Same did not differ at all, then whenever something became the same, it would always become one, and whenever one, the same.

I take it that (1) and (2) together indicate that there are counterexamples that defeat any proposed identity between the natures of The
One and The Same, and that (3) holds in virtue of the general rule
that when natures are the same they must share all instances. It therefore follows from these considerations that the natures of The Same
and The One are not the same (the result stated at 139d2–3). If we
take this to be sufficient to show that The One is not the same *pros
heauto,* then we can go on to apply the transitivity rule, concluding
finally that The One cannot be the same as itself *pros heauto* (the
conclusion announced at 139d1, repeated with other results in the
summary at 139e4–5).[9]

Now that we see how the overall argument of this passage works
and how the subargument fits within it, our only remaining task is to
evaluate the claim in the subargument about the counterexamples. Notice that we need examples of becoming the same with many in a
rather strong sense. That is

   What becomes the same as many must become many

is not enough, since being many does not automatically exclude being
one; for all this says, there might not be any cases where what is the
same is not one. The cases being entertained must resist being taken
as unities, and the claim must be that in such cases:

   What becomes the same as many must become many *and not* be-
      come one.

This is exactly what our text says (139d4–5).

Let us see whether we can develop an example that plausibly contains a many in this strong sense. Consider the case in which the three
smallest cats become the three best-fed cats (which is a case of becoming the same with many, at least in one sense). Have the three smallest
cats in this case become one? It is possible to say "No." After all,
our three small cats were not one before, and merely coinciding with
the three best-fed cats does not seem capable of introducing unity where
there was none before. A philosophical reason to serve as a backing
for this intuition could be as follows: we can only speak of something
as one against a background that provides an answer to the question:
one *what?*[10] Because there are cases where there is no possibility of
providing an answer to the question, there are cases of coinciding—
that is, of being the same—that are not cases of being one.

This shows that there does seem to be a class of cases of the kind we need—cases in which what becomes the same does not become one. I take

(2) Τοῖς πολλοῖς ταὐτὸν γενόμενον πολλὰ ἀνάγκη γίγνεσθαι ἀλλ' οὐχ ἕν. (139d4–5)

(2) Becoming the same with many, it must become many, not one

to be indicating this class, and so to accomplish what the overall argument as I explained it demands.

Understanding this passage in the way I have recommended, however, does have one impediment. The use of singular forms in

ἐπειδὰν ταὐτὸν γένηταί τῳ τι (139d3)

and

Τοῖς πολλοῖς ταὐτὸν γενόμενον (139d4–5)

does seem to presuppose some unity in what becomes the same. This problem is softened somewhat by the circumstance that the indefinite article brings these singular forms into the sentence, and it is perhaps indefinite enough to be applicable precisely in cases where the question, "One what?" remains unanswerable. All of the other singular forms would then be for the sake of syntactic propriety, and without further significance.

The arguments at 139e7–140b5 have the key words *chōris* (separate from) and *phusis* (nature) in them, and so seem to invite construal on the lines I have been developing. Discussing which natures are separate is just what someone engaged in inquiry into what holds of a subject in relation to itself should be doing; when we find that a nature is separate from our subject's nature, we know that the associated *pros heauto* predication does not hold.

The passage falls into two parts: from 139e7–140a6 establishes that The One is not like itself or another, and 140a6–b5 that it is not unlike itself or another. Since I think that the second part repeats the strategy of the first, I will discuss explicitly only 139e7–140a6. This passage will turn out not only to invite construal on the lines I have been developing, but also to have no other natural construal that yields a good argument. Here, as in the case of the passage I just finished

discussing, I will start by saying how I understand the passage. By
this time, it will perhaps not be necessary to state explicitly what other
options are available and why I do not choose them.

The passage opens by introducing the results it seeks to establish:

Οὐδὲ μὴν ὅμοιόν τινι ἔσται οὐδ' ἀνόμοιον οὔτε αὑτῷ οὔτε ἑτέρῳ.
(139e7–8)

Nor will it be like or unlike itself or another.

Next, as I understand the text, comes the account of Likeness to be
used in the first argument (which will deal with whether The One is
like itself or another). This is:

τὸ ταὐτόν που πεπονθὸς ὅμοιον. (139e8)

Likeness is having suffered the same (i.e., to be like is to have suffered
the same).[11]

We are then reminded that Same is no part of the nature of The One:

Τοῦ δέ γε ἑνὸς χωρὶς ἐφάνη τὴν φύσιν τὸ ταὐτόν. (139e9–140a1)

The Same appeared separate in nature from The One.

This gives us enough to derive our result by an application of the
transitivity rule, as follows:

Same is in the account of Like.

But Same is not in the account of One.

So Like cannot be predicated *pros heauto* of The One.

The problematic detail about understanding this passage is what to
do with:

Ἀλλὰ μὴν εἴ τι πέπονθε χωρὶς τοῦ ἓν εἶναι τὸ ἕν, πλείω ἂν
εἶναι πεπόνθοι ἢ ἕν, τοῦτο δὲ ἀδύνατον. (140a1–3)

But if The One had suffered ⟨being⟩ anything separate from being one,
it would suffer being more than one, but that is impossible.

In fact, construal of this as reasonable will yield a reading that fits
well with the overall argument I just sketched. There are of course
various ways of construing the sentence now in question. At this point,

it may be too tedious to go through all those I reject, so I will simply state my construal of it and leave it to readers who wish to do so to observe how implausible the sentence is on any reading that is substantially different.

I believe that this sentence intends us to consider what it would mean to suppose that The One was *pros heauto* anything separate from being one (first clause).[12] Such a predication would attribute to The One a nature that was separate from its original nature—that is, The One would have two distinct natures (second clause). What is crucial here is the word "separate." Although it is possible to attribute to The Cat a nature not identical with Cathood—for example, Animality— Cat and Animal are not *separate:* they stand in a part-whole relation, and so are not disjoint. Thus the predicate in question does not give The Cat two distinct natures. But to predicate of The One something that was separate from its original nature would give it two distinct natures. The sentence ends (third clause) by proclaiming this to be impossible. And rightly so.[13]

This concludes my comments on details of the passage. The two arguments of the passage, as I construe them, have turned out to follow a strategy outlined already for others that appeared earlier in the section, but with an added consideration. This consideration establishes a plausible claim about natures: a thing cannot have predicates *pros heauto* that are separate from the thing's own nature.

A familiar feature of the *Parmenides* is that some of its arguments have seemed extremely bad. The range of responses of commentators to this is also familiar. They may omit to discuss such passages, or claim that Plato was simply mistaken in thinking his arguments to be good, or that he thought giving bad arguments to be a good joke. They may also find ways of characterizing Plato's purpose in such a way that would make the arguments appropriate. We have discussed the two major ways of doing this; they are, first, to suppose that Plato meant each "bad" argument as a *reductio,* and second, to introduce special subjects for the arguments, with the thought that the results (or the arguments at least) would be proper, when understood as applying to those special subjects. Of all of these strategies, only the last seems to me to have any promise. And, as we have seen, it has no small drawbacks. Some problems at the general level were mentioned in chapter 1. And as we have been seeing in the present chapter, it does not make as much sense of the arguments in the text as one would have hoped.

Our interpretation of the first section of the gymnastic dialectic has given the arguments that had seemed to be most appallingly bad a reasonable construal without being forced to take some previously sound-seeming argument as correspondingly confused. The readings found for the arguments, which individually recommended themselves to me by seeming to make the arguments reasonable, have a further interesting feature: they give to each of these arguments the purpose of establishing that some nature is no part of the nature of The One. This purpose can be shared by all the arguments in the section—that is, by the ones I did not discuss explicitly, as well as by those I did.

This confirms my expectation that this first section of arguments is a response to the theme question: if The One is, what follows for The One in relation to itself?[14] Given this shared overall purpose, the particular arguments differ in procedure and in emphasis. Some rely on the evidence of the claim once it is asserted; some discredit the candidate nature by showing that it involves another that has already been excluded; one goes through a test for nonidentity of natures from inspection of particulars: natures with unshared instances are not the same; and one makes explicit that a thing cannot have as a *pros heauto* predicate anything separate from its nature.

5

The Second Section of Arguments

We come now to the second section of arguments constituting Parmenides' dialectical display. As we have already noted in our inquiry into the structure of the exercise, this section is explicitly devoted to determining what follows for The One, if The One is. In fact, I expect that the "theme question" of the section can be more completely expressed as follows: what follows for The One *pros ta alla,* if The One is? (For both points, see chapter 2.) The business of this chapter is to confirm that this expectation is fulfilled. To do this, I will first explore further than I have yet done the class of predications *pros ta alla.* This exploration will make it possible to see what sort of activities would be involved in establishing such predications and so in answering the proposed theme question. Then, I will show how we can understand the arguments of the section as carrying out those activities. (I will not discuss every argument individually, but will take up some representative ones.) I would like to start this chapter, however, by providing a summary of the second section proper and the interpretative issues it raises.

Issues in Interpreting the Second Section

Now that we are looking in greater detail at this section by itself, we are faced with a complication I have not yet mentioned. Although I have discussed the issue of the apparent contradictions between the conclusions of *different* sections, there has as yet been no occasion to consider the issue of tension or incoherence of paired results *within* a single section. The second section offers such an occasion. In predi-

cating opposites and even contradictories of The One, it repeats in
small the puzzling pattern of results of the dialectic as a whole.

We can give a cautious summary of the results of the section—that
is, one that is neutral between interpretations—as follows. The predicates whose application to The One the section considers are the same
that were in question in the first section of arguments. However, where
the first section denied all of the candidate predicates to The One, the
arguments of the second section jointly apply them all, even though
some are the opposites of others; they also go on, in some cases, to
apply the contradictory of a term that has already been asserted to hold
of The One. Thus, we find among the conclusions of these arguments
that The One is one and many, is in motion and at rest, has limit and
is unlimited, is the same and different, is becoming younger than the
others and not becoming younger than the others, and so on.

Despite this superficially bizarre pattern of results, this section has
had a much less colorful history than the first section had. We have
seen that, in their struggle to explicate the results of the first section,
commentators developed a range of interpretations. These vary in the
sense they give to the section's conclusions, as well as in the strategy
they attribute to Plato (to demonstrate the conclusions, or to use them
in the course of a *reductio*). By contrast, in the case of the second
section, there seems to be, roughly speaking, agreement on the sense
of the conclusions, with disagreement only on whether these results
are acceptable and meant as such or have a role within a *reductio* of
their own. I will now sketch my construal of the conclusions of the
section, indicating how my interpretation is related to others. Then I
will go on to explain the issue of the acceptability of the results so
construed.

My reading of these conclusions is, again roughly speaking, the
standard reading. My understanding of the methodological remarks leads
me to expect that this section will investigate what results for The One
pros ta alla, if The One is. Study of the passage itself will confirm
that this characterization indeed fits the section. Although I will differ
from other commentators in describing the section as achieving results
pros ta alla, this will not lead to the kind of divergence from their
understanding of the results that occurred with the corresponding claim
that the first section achieved results *pros heauto.*

This is because getting results for The One *pros ta alla,* as I understand it, involves finding out what features The One displays, and this

is what readers have always understood the section as doing. Thus, for example, when we read in this section "The One is the same as itself," I join others in taking this to mean that The One displays Self-Identity.[1] We can describe the situation from within my scheme by noting that, since people have (without thinking of themselves as doing so) been taking *all* predications as predications *pros ta alla,* their understanding of results that I too take as *pros ta alla* agrees with mine, whereas we diverge where I take results as really predications *pros heauto.* Hence my greater divergence from others over the first section, when compared with the second. This pattern will be continued with later sections.

Despite the general agreement over the force of the conclusions of this section, some disagreement persists over whether Plato meant to present these conclusions as problematic and so as part of another *reductio,* or whether he instead meant them to stand as established. But here (and this is one manifestation of the negligible strangeness of this section compared with the first) the results taken individually do not seem very problematic. The results only seem problematic when looked at as part of certain larger patterns. Let us take these patterns one at a time.

As I mentioned previously, the section's conclusions attribute opposite pairs of predicates, and even contradictory pairs of predicates, to its subject. This pattern may be thought to present two distinct problems, though I think we can ultimately dismiss both.

The first problem would arise if these results cannot all hold at once, that is, if there is unacceptable tension between them. In fact, some do feel that the section's pattern of results is straightforwardly incoherent and logically unacceptable.[2] This unacceptability is then supposed to be our cue to view the section as having a *reductio*-oriented strategy. Yet our passage's results (and manner of arguing for them) seem to repeat faithfully a pattern that the middle dialogues had accustomed us to think of as characteristically Platonic, and which readers of the middle dialogues have never tried to reject.[3] The fifth book of the *Republic* contains perhaps the most famous of these passages. Plato there described sensible particulars as "rolling about between being and not being" precisely because, although they exhibited certain features in a way, in some relation, or at a time, they also failed to exhibit those features (or exhibited the opposite features) in some other connection.[4] (The *Republic* passage occupies roughly the last six

Stephanus pages of this book. Cf. *Phaedo* 74a9 ff. and *Symposium* 210e2 ff.) At one level, this is just the kind of result that the second section of the *Parmenides* also generates: the pattern of predicates in question is the same. I will, in this chapter, discuss a representative pair of arguments from this section of the *Parmenides* whose results might seem incompatible. In fact, the discussion will show that there is no logical problem here, for the same reason that there is none in the *Republic* passage.

The next reason for finding the section's combined results unacceptable has to do not with the logical status of the results but with their "lack of fit" with other famous Platonic tenets. In fact, the very passages from the middle dialogues to which I just likened ours do differ from it in one important respect. The pattern of predicates attributed in the passages is indeed the same. But there is a change in the *subject* of the predicates in question. In the middle dialogues, this pattern of predicates was attributed only to sensible particulars, which were notoriously supposed to contrast with forms. Forms were whatever they were purely and without qualification. Now we can see that our passage—in saying The One is one and many, becomes and does not become younger than the others—does not just repeat a familiar Platonic refrain. For since Parmenides' methodological remarks implied that the subjects for his dialectical exercise were forms, The One must be a form; that is, The One belongs precisely to the class that in the middle dialogues was exempt from the "rolling about."

Now clearly, the "lack of fit" between the results of our passage and the relevant ones from the middle dialogues need not mean that the results of our passage are to be rejected. The alternative possibility that Plato's views on this point evolved is worth considering (especially because of the two circumstances that the picture of forms in the middle dialogues, if taken strictly, has always appeared problematic; and that there is abundant evidence that we are not supposed to reject the conclusions of Parmenides' dialectic). In fact, we will be able to dismiss the other lines of thought suggesting rejection of these results. The "lack of fit" standing by itself will then have to be taken as a sign of Plato's modification of his views; it alone is not enough to make rejectionism our interpretative attitude to the *Parmenides*.

If Plato did change his views on this matter, it was no trivial change. For the contrast between the rolling about of sensible particulars with the pure Being of the forms was associated with fundamental tenets of the metaphysics and epistemology of the middle dialogues. That is, it was connected with the status of forms as truly real, whereas sensible particulars were ontologically dependent on them, as well as with the doctrine that forms only were the objects of knowledge, whereas sensible particulars were the objects of opinion. Thus, if Plato indeed increased the population that rolls about, it will be interesting to consider the corresponding changes in his views on knowledge and opinion, as well as on the ontological priority of forms. I will turn to these issues in my final chapter. For the moment, we may keep this in mind as adding interest to our immediate project of making sense of the second section of arguments: we should not choose a developmental story without having first determined the basic issues of the sense of the conclusions of this section and Plato's strategy in deriving them.

We have now discussed the two reasons for finding unacceptable the pattern of combined results of the second section of arguments. A second grouping, that of this section with the first, can be laid aside since it does not affect the acceptability of our section's results. That is, perceived contradiction between the results of the two sections has had little influence on the interpretation of the second section. The majority of readers reject the results of the first section of arguments, so that maintaining compatibility with those results is not an issue for them. Those who do not do this, so far as I know, interpret the first and second sections in such a way that the results of one section are not "in logical contact" with those of the other. Thus, for all readers, if any results of the second section are to be rejected, it will not be to remove results repugnant in connection with the achievements of the prior section, but for some other reason.

I hope that this preliminary discussion of the interpretative issues connected with the section has clarified the larger issues related to our coming inquiry. We can now turn to the job of arriving at a basic understanding of the section: determining what its conclusions mean, and whether they are to be accepted. My exploration of results *pros ta alla* will be a preparation for turning to the text, giving us a precise idea of what to expect, which can then be confirmed or rejected by seeing whether it fits the text. Because the passage is long, I will not look at every argument individually but will discuss generally the procedures I expect to find followed in the section, and then show how they are followed in the cases of some representative arguments. This will indicate sufficiently how I take the rest of the section.

My choice of these representative arguments has not been determined wholly by their being able to be explicated as deriving results
for The One *pros ta alla*—that is true of all the arguments in the
section. I have chosen them for their additional interest. I chose the
first pair of arguments because of a certain special problem associated
with them. They are two demonstrations, each concluding that The
One is unlimited *(apeiron)*. This has led to various opinions concerning whether the two arguments in fact establish the same thing, or are
complementary in some way. Reflections I will make in connection
with my scheme will help lead to a new answer to this problem.[5] I
chose my second pair for its bearing on the issue of whether there is
tension between results within the section: I will undertake to show
why a representative result of the form "The One is F and not F," as
Plato derives it here, is unproblematically true.

Further Analysis of *Pros Ta Alla* Results

Our first task now is to reflect in greater detail on the character of
results *pros ta alla*. Equipped with a fuller understanding of them, we
can see how to determine when they hold and then check that the
second section of Parmenides' dialectic does carry out the kind of
activities we anticipate.

We can use two observations as a starting point. The first concerns
Parmenides' methodological remarks, now so familiar to us. While
these remarks were initially not transparent, even when not understood, they conveyed an impression of extreme comprehensiveness.
Thus, there is a presumption that the *pros heauto* and *pros ta alla*
truths about something, taken together, will be all the truths that there
are about that thing. The second observation we start with derives
from our first investigations of predication *pros ta alla* (chapter 3).
There, certain suggestive passages from the fifth section of arguments,
dealing with The One's being unlike and unequal, indicated that the
pros ta alla results for something include results we characterized non-
technically as concerning the display of features by the thing; we then
developed a Platonic analysis of this as involving exhibiting or con-
forming to a property. But are these all the *pros ta alla* results concerning that thing?

We can start to see that the class of *pros ta alla* results concerning something should include more than just these, by using our first observation, that the *pros heauto* and *pros ta alla* results concerning a subject between them are all the truths about that subject. Let us take as an example Justice, and collect a group of truths about it that are clearly not *pros heauto*. We can therefore expect them to be in the *pros ta alla* class. Let us start with the following:

(1) Justice is eternal.

(2) Justice is one.

(3) Socrates displays Justice.

(4) Justice is exhibited twice in the Antipodes.

As we will see, there is an important difference among these: they do not all involve Justice's exhibiting a feature; rather, (1) and (2) will be true in virtue of Justice's exhibiting a feature, while (3) and (4) are based on *other entities exhibiting Justice*.

This grouping may at first seem surprising. If we let ourselves be guided by the superficial grammatical structure of the sentences, then (1), (2), and (4) all seem to go together. So let us consider briefly the question of the basis for analysis and categorization we should expect Plato to use (grammatical structure or something else). As soon as we put the question, the answer becomes obvious: Plato is not interested in the superficial grammatical form of sentences, but in the *onta* (which I shall be calling "facts" or "states of affairs") in virtue of which they are asserted. This is not a distinction without a difference: there is not a one–one pairing of sentences with associated facts.

Consider that, for example,

(3) Socrates displays Justice

and

(3′) Justice is displayed by Socrates

differ in their superficial grammatical structure but hold in virtue of the same fact. So a single fact can be expressed by several sentences. We also know that a single sentence may be used in virtue of each of several states of affairs. Two kinds of example are in place here. First, homonymy can result in a single sentence's being able to express more than one fact (unless "sentence" is taken so that the presence of homonyms distinguishes sentences that appear the same). Second, our own inquiry makes clear to us that, in Plato's view, some sentences can be asserted in virtue of distinct states of affairs. This is, of course, because of Plato's use of two kinds of predication. Thus,

    The One is not green

can be asserted either in virtue of the fact that being green is no part of being one, or of the distinct fact that the individual, The One, is not colored green. Given that sentences of different structures may be associated with a single fact, and that a single sentence can be associated with facts of different kinds, we can see that the structures of sentences and associated facts can come apart: otherwise, only one kind of sentence could go with a given fact, and vice versa.

Now, since we are interested in analyzing and categorizing our *pros ta alla* results on the basis of the facts involved, and since we have established that we cannot determine the structure of these facts on the basis of the grammatical structure of the sentences involved, we will have to investigate the facts themselves further. We know it is characteristic of Plato's program to expect that one way of describing these states of affairs (or the basic ones among them) is to say that they involve things participating in forms; however, we have established that it is part of the message of the *Parmenides* that the participation relation is not adequately understood. So, rather than invoking participation now, we will pursue the other direction. After establishing what relations ground predications *pros ta alla* and predications *pros heauto* (i.e., all true subject-predicate sentences), we will be in a position to reconstruct the notion of participation.

We may, however, start with the relation I have been calling displaying or exhibiting. Our examination (in chapter 3) of passages from the dialogue has already established that at least some results *pros ta alla* involve the subject's displaying properties. We will therefore be proceeding conservatively if we determine whether we can account for all predications *pros ta alla* by use of this relation. (I will represent the displaying relation by means of the two-place predicate Displays (X, Y), where X is the displayer and Y is displayed.) Let us look now at our four sample *pros ta alla* assertions about Justice.

It is straightforward enough to say that

    (1) Justice is eternal

holds in virtue of the fact

Displays (Justice, Eternality).

Similarly,

(2) Justice is one

holds because of the obtaining of the fact

Displays (Justice, Unity).

When we come to (3), though, we find something a little different. We can easily dispel any temptation to toy with the idea that

(3) Justice is displayed by Socrates

holds in virtue of the putative fact

Displays (Justice, Being-Displayed-by-Socrates).

We recollect that we wanted to recognize (3) as being equivalent to:

(3′) Socrates displays Justice.

What the recognition of the equivalence suggests is that we take the grounding of (3) to be the same as that of (3′), namely:

Displays (Socrates, Justice).

(Notice that we do *not* want:

Displays (Socrates, Display-of-Justice).

This invites intolerable regress.)

(3) thus turns out to be grounded by a fact in which Justice is the second rather than the first term related by the displaying relation— that is, Justice is itself displayed rather than displaying. This is our first example of a sentence used to express a *pros ta alla* result that is not grounded in the grammatical subject's displaying a property. In this case the reason is simple. The grammatical structure, with its passive construction, determines the subject of the sentence: "Justice" rather than "Socrates" is the subject of the passive verb. Nevertheless, we are still dealing with a case in which the displayer and the displayed (Socrates and Justice) are both named in the sentence.

What is more interesting is that this need not be so. To see this let us go on to:

(4) Justice is displayed twice in the Antipodes.

When we ask ourselves about the facts grounding this, we can see
again that there are two possible answers: one that follows the grammatical structure of the sentence and another that takes further the sort
of analysis we have begun to develop. The first answer, that is, takes
its starting point from the observation that "Justice" is the grammatical subject of this subject-predicate sentence. This can lead to thinking
the sentence is grounded in the fact:

   Displays (Justice, Being-Displayed-Twice-in-the-Antipodes).

The pile-up here of displayings is clearly inelegant. But here, we
cannot just simplemindedly follow the strategy we used in the case of
(3). The closest we can come to the manipulation that succeeded with
(3) would in the present case be

   Displays (Twice-in-the-Antipodes, Justice),

which is not quite what we want. What we do want (in case Smith
and Jones are two just Antipodeans) is:

   Displays (Smith, Justice)

   Displays (Jones, Justice).

(We want either these two facts, or some sort of complex fact. For
purposes of our present concerns we do not need to go into this difficult issue.)

   There are two important things to note here. First, what this analysis
puts forward as the ultimate grounding of (4), as of (3), are facts in
which Justice is the second rather than the first term related by the
displaying relation; this shows an important subdivision within our
sample sentences, since no such treatment of (1) and (2) is available.
Second, the facts that ground (4) are ones in which the first terms are
entities whose names did not appear in sentence (4) at all. Although I
do not wish to belabor the point, it should be clear that, far from being
the only sentence of this kind, (4) is representative of a whole group.
That is, such *pros ta alla* assertions as

   (5) Justice is rare in the Antipodes

   (6) Health is commoner than Justice

also fulfill the two conditions elaborated in connection with (4): the
facts that ground them are ones in which Justice is the second term in

the displaying relation,[6] and the first terms do not appear explicitly in the sentences.

Let us sum up what we have determined so far. We have indeed been able to use facts involving the displaying relation in analyzing all our sample *pros ta alla* results about Justice. However, we have found also a division within the group. In some cases, the facts that ground the assertions are of the form

Displays (Justice, ———);

in others they are of the form

Displays (———, Justice).

That is, given that we have identified Justice as the thing about which we are collecting truths *pros ta alla,* those truths are grounded in two kinds of facts: facts in which Justice displays something, and facts in which things display Justice. These have in common that both fall under the schema

Displays (———, ———);

they differ in whether Justice is the first or second term in the relation. Our fact-oriented analysis has therefore shown us both what is common to assertions *pros ta alla* and an important principle of division within the group. Soon we will see how this distinction within the group of *pros ta alla* results manifests itself in our text.

On Establishing *Pros Ta Alla* Results

As a final preparation before returning to the text, let us think about how someone could set about obtaining *pros ta alla* results, as we understand them. I will first describe what seems intuitively to be one kind of appropriate procedure, and then show how we can describe that procedure in terms we have already developed in connection with the scheme of the *Parmenides.*

Let us suppose that someone seeks to show that some state s is an aristocracy. Let us further suppose that the correct account of Aristocracy is:

Aristocracy is rule of the best.

Clearly, it is sufficient to establish the desired result to show that, in s, the best indeed rule: this shows s satisfies the account.

Now let us try to describe this procedure in terms native to the *Parmenides*. Since the account of Aristocracy I just invoked is clearly its *pros heauto* characterization, we are envisaging a role for *pros heauto* truths in establishing *pros ta alla* ones. (They are playing the role that definitions have in some other schemes.) The procedure works as follows. Our investigator, in observing that in s the best indeed rule, is showing that s displays what is on the right-hand side of the account. Now since the account is a kind of identity statement, s will also display what is on the left-hand side of the account, which is what we need to establish in order to justify the *pros ta alla* assertion: s is an aristocracy.

Someone might be worried at the suggestion that a state s could be said to satisfy the account of Aristocracy. The worry would be that, in a Platonic context, only Aristocracy itself should be allowed to satisfy the account of Aristocracy, since it alone is the very thing of which the account is an account. The key point in understanding why we need not worry is that, in the scheme of the *Parmenides*, state s on the one hand and Aristocracy on the other have very different relations to what is specified in the account. A state satisfies the account by *displaying or exhibiting* rule of the best, perhaps even by doing so perfectly. The state is not even trying to *be* rule of the best: of course, it could not aspire to be a property, nor need it since we are dealing with predication *pros ta alla* here. Nor does Aristocracy, in order to be the property, need to display rule of the best as a feature. In the dialogue's terms, Aristocracy is rule of the best *pros heauto*, not *pros ta alla*.

This first example involved an empirical step (looking at the world to see who ruled in s). But we can see that not all such demonstrations need do. Consider the case of someone who wishes to show that some continuous magnitude m is *apeiron plēthei* (unlimited in multitude). He can do so by showing that m has a series of parts a, b, c, . . . that goes on without limit, and then appeal to the account of *apeiron plēthei*.

Now that we have identified a general procedure for establishing *pros ta alla* results, we can easily see how the difference between the two kinds of *pros ta alla* assertions concerning a subject will manifest itself. We may start by noting that an assertion does not have either character in isolation, but only in the context of an inquiry where something has already been identified as the subject. That is, it is a matter of there being different kinds of facts *concerning a subject* rather than of there being different kinds of facts *tout court*.[7] Given that some inquiry has subject F, the two kinds of fact about it are those of the form

(i) Displays (F, ———)

and those of the form

(ii) Displays (———, F).

We can establish these by the general procedure suggested by the first two examples. If the fact in question is of type (i), we take the account of the second term and show that F satisfies it; if it is, on the other hand, of type (ii), we take the account of F and show that the first term satisfies it. Our discussion has shown that whether the fact we are interested in is of type (i) or type (ii) is independent of the grammatical structure of the sentence that expresses the fact; we have paid special attention to cases in which the facts to be established are of type (ii), although the sentences expressing them do not suggest this by *their* structure (and indeed make no explicit mention of the entities whose place is held in schema (ii) by "———").

Now that we have explored one type of procedure for establishing results *pros ta alla,* we can note briefly that we need not expect all the arguments in our section to follow it. Given that some results have been established, we can anticipate a kind of proof that takes its starting point from prior results within the section. For we might take ourselves to know, in some cases, that a feature P must be accompanied by another feature Q. In such cases, once we have proved that our subject is P *pros ta alla,* we can conclude that it also has Q as a *pros ta alla* predicate. In fact, this type of argument is very common in the section.

Discussion of Arguments from the Text: First Pair

We are now ready to turn to the first pair of passages that I have selected for discussion. They are the two demonstrations that The One is *apeiron* (142d9–143a3 and 144c2–e7; the second passage is indeed

only the final stage of an argument that starts at 143a4). This is the
only example in the dialectic of two arguments within a single section
apparently to the same conclusion, and commentators have produced
a variety of explanations for this. Of course at the broadest level, the
two explanatory options are that the two arguments achieve identical
results, one being just extra, or that their results differ in some way.
Within the second option, one may choose from a variety of ways in
which the two proofs may be thought to differ. The appearance in the
text of the distinct phrases *to hen on* and *auto to hen* may be thought
to suggest that the two deal with different subjects. (This issue is very
difficult to explore because of serious textual problems at crucial points).
Another suggestion (offered by Sayre)[8] is that the first proof shows
that Unity yields *numberless* multitude; this result is then used in proving the existence of number, leading finally to the conclusion of the
second proof, that Unity is indefinitely *numerous*.

To settle every difficulty about this pair of passages seems to me to
be an impossible task. However, that is not necessary for the present
purpose, which is simply to confirm that the undertakings of the second section of arguments are of the sort our understanding of Parmenides' methodological remarks leads us to expect. What I would like
to do now is to show how the proceedings in this pair of demonstrations lend themselves to being characterized in the terms that emerged
in the discussion of investigation into results *pros ta alla* just preceding: I will show how we can see the two as establishing results
concerning the displays of features, but differing in whether The One
is displayer or displayed.

The first demonstration picks up on the result (established at 142c7–
d5) that if The One is, then it has parts, its Unity and Being. It then
runs on:

Τί οὖν; τῶν μορίων ἑκάτερον τούτων τοῦ ἑνὸς ὄντος, τό τε ἓν καὶ
τὸ ὄν, ἆρα ἀπολείπεσθον ἢ τὸ ἓν τοῦ εἶναι μορίου ἢ τὸ ὂν τοῦ
ἑνὸς μορίου;—Οὐκ ἂν εἴη.—Πάλιν ἄρα καὶ τῶν μορίων ἑκάτερον
τό τε ἓν ἴσχει καὶ τὸ ὄν, καὶ γίγνεται τὸ ἐλάχιστον ἐκ δυοῖν αὖ
μορίοιν τὸ μόριον, καὶ κατὰ τὸν αὐτὸν λόγον οὕτως ἀεί, ὅτιπερ
ἂν μόριον γένηται, τούτω τὼ μορίω ἀεὶ ἴσχει· τό τε γὰρ ἓν τὸ ὂν
ἀεὶ ἴσχει καὶ τὸ ὂν τὸ ἕν· ὥστε ἀνάγκη δύ᾽ ἀεὶ γιγνόμενον μηδέ-
ποτε ἓν εἶναι.—Παντάπασι μὲν οὖν.—Οὐκοῦν ἄπειρον ἂν τὸ
πλῆθος οὕτω τὸ ἓν ὂν εἴη;—Ἔοικεν. (142d9–143a3)

What now? Concerning each of these parts of The One that is, Being and Unity, is Unity lacking from the part Being or Being from the part Unity?—It wouldn't be.—So each of the parts in turn has both Unity and Being, and the part turns out to come from at least[9] two parts, and so on forever by the same reasoning: whatever part comes about, always has this pair of parts. For Unity always has Being and Being Unity. So that ⟨any part⟩ must, always becoming two, never be one.— Very much so.—So The One that is would thus be unlimited in multitude?—It seems so.

The second demonstration proceeds from two preliminary results. The first is the so-called generation of number. The next is that Being is infinitely divided, since a part of it must go to each number. Now our passage goes on as follows. (Because this passage presents several textual problems and requires interpretation by translators, it is unwise to rely heavily on the details of any one presentation as authoritative.)

Τί οὖν; ἔστι τι αὐτῶν ὃ ἔστι μὲν μέρος τῆς οὐσίας, οὐδὲν μέντοι μέρος;—Καὶ πῶς ἄν [τοι] τοῦτο γένοιτο;—Ἀλλ᾽ εἴπερ γε οἶμαι ἔστιν, ἀνάγκη αὐτὸ ἀεί, ἕωσπερ ἂν ᾖ, ἕν γέ τι εἶναι, μηδὲν δὲ ἀδύνατον.—Ἀνάγκη.—Πρὸς ἅπαντι ἄρα [ἑκάστῳ] τῷ τῆς οὐσίας μέρει πρόσεστιν τὸ ἕν, οὐκ ἀπολειπόμενον οὔτε σμικροτέρου οὔτε μείζονος μέρους οὔτε ἄλλου οὐδενός.—Οὕτω.—Ἆρα οὖν ἓν ὂν πολλαχοῦ ἅμα ὅλον ἐστί; τοῦτο ἄθρει.—Ἀλλ᾽ ἀθρῶ καὶ ὁρῶ ὅτι ἀδύνατον.—Μεμερισμένον ἄρα, εἴπερ μὴ ὅλον· ἄλλως γάρ που οὐδαμῶς ἅμα ἅπασι τοῖς τῆς οὐσίας μέρεσιν παρέσται ἢ μεμερισμένον.—Ναί.—Καὶ μὴν τό γε μεριστὸν πολλὴ ἀνάγκη εἶναι τοσαῦτα ὅσαπερ μέρη.—Ἀνάγκη.—Οὐκ ἄρα ἀληθῆ ἄρτι ἐλέγομεν λέγοντες ὡς πλεῖστα μέρη ἡ οὐσία νενεμημένη εἴη. οὐδὲ γὰρ πλείω τοῦ ἑνὸς νενέμηται, ἀλλ᾽ ἴσα, ὡς ἔοικε, τῷ ἑνί· οὔτε γὰρ τὸ ὂν τοῦ ἑνὸς ἀπολείπεται οὔτε τὸ ἓν τοῦ ὄντος, ἀλλ᾽ ἐξισοῦσθον δύο ὄντε ἀεὶ παρὰ πάντα.—Παντάπασιν οὕτω φαίνεται.—Τὸ ἓν ἄρα αὐτὸ κεκερματισμένον ὑπὸ τῆς οὐσίας πολλά τε καὶ ἄπειρα τὸ πλῆθός ἐστιν.—Φαίνεται.—Οὐ μόνον ἄρα τὸ ὂν ἓν πολλά ἐστιν, ἀλλὰ καὶ αὐτὸ τὸ ἓν ὑπὸ τοῦ ὄντος διανενεμημένον πολλὰ ἀνάγκη εἶναι.—Παντάπασι μὲν οὖν. (144c2–e7)

What now? Is there any one of them that is a part of Being, but no part?—How could there be?—But I suppose if it is, it must always, while it is, be some one thing; it cannot be nothing.—Necessarily.—So Unity is present to every part of Being, lacking neither to a small part nor to a large part nor to any other.—It is so.—Well, being one is it in many places at the same time as a whole? Examine that.—I do examine it, and I see that it is impossible.—And if not as a whole, then it is divided, for I suppose in no other way will it be present at the same time to all the parts of Being than being divided.—No.—And what is divided must be as numerous as its parts.—Necessarily.—Then we did not speak truly just now when we said that Being was distributed in the greatest number of parts. For it isn't distributed in more ⟨parts⟩ than The One, but in an equal number, it seems, with The One. For what is does not lack Unity nor does what is one lack Being, but being two they are equal in all things.—It certainly seems so.—The One itself therefore, minced up by Being, is many and unlimited in multitude.— It seems so.—Then not only is The One that is many but also The One itself must be many since it is distributed by Being.—Very much so.[10]

One perennial question about these two demonstrations, as I mentioned earlier, concerns their relation to each other. Is the second redundant, or do the two prove distinct results? We can now begin to answer this question in terms of our investigations into the internal division within the group of *pros ta alla* results: each argument will be seen to deal with one of the two kinds of result.

The first passage seems clearly to be undertaking the same task concerning The One that I outlined in my example of someone demonstrating that some continuous magnitude m was *apeiron plēthei*. The idea there was that m had parts and that these were infinitely numerous. Having such parts is being *apeiron plēthei,* so demonstrating the existence of that series of parts was demonstrating that the fact .

Displays (m, The *apeiron*)

held. It is important to note that the parts a, b, c . . . of m were precisely not of such a kind that

Displays (a, M-ness)

Displays (b, M-ness)

Displays (c, M-ness)

and so on

held,[11] so a *fortiori* those were not the facts that grounded the assertion. That is, this was what I called a type (i) rather that a type (ii) situation: a situation concerning the subject as the first, rather than the second term, in the displaying relation.

The first demonstration that The One is *apeiron* clearly demonstrates its conclusion in just the same way. It shows the existence of an infinitely extended series of parts of The One (its Being and Unity, their Being and Unity, the Being and Unity of those . . .) that are not introduced as participants, but just as ordinary parts. Since having such a series of parts is being *apeiron plēthei*, this shows that

Displays (The One, The *apeiron*)

holds. Thus, we have a fact concerning our subject as displaying, and so we might say that, in virtue of this, The One is *apeiron* in a direct sense.

We are now ready to turn to the second demonstration, which we might describe as showing that the same predicate holds of The One indirectly. We saw earlier that when the facts

Displays (Smith, Justice)

Displays (Jones, Justice)

hold, they may be the grounding for the assertion:

Justice is displayed twice in the Antipodes.

Here there is a sense in which Justice does not display anything directly. Rather, the attribution of a grammatical predicate to "Justice" as grammatical subject is legitimate as a summary or reflection of certain facts in which subjects unnamed in the sentence display Justice. We might perhaps say that in such a case the predicate holds of Justice indirectly.

Now, clearly there was nothing special in the circumstance that I supposed Justice to be displayed twice. That is, we can easily see the possibility of summary attributions reflecting a larger, even unlimited number of displays. And an unlimited number of displays of Unity is indeed what our demonstration treats. It is somewhat difficult to keep track of the direct/indirect distinction here, since the series

Displays (2, Unity)

Displays (3, Unity)

Displays (4, Unity)

and so on

that grounds the reflective or summary assertion

The One is *apeiron*

and hence the indirect ascription of *apeiron* to The One has a certain similarity to the series that grounded the direct ascription of *apeiron* to The One, which we have just been considering: it also goes on without end. But the crucial difference is that this series is a series of facts in which Unity is displayed; the series grounding the direct ascription of *apeiron* to The One was a series of parts of Unity. Indeed, if the things doing the displaying turn out to be parts in an appropriate sense, the present series would yield a series of parts that could be used in a proof that

The One is *apeiron*

obtains directly. However, independently of that, the existence of the series of numbers each of which displays Unity grounds the summary assertion

The One is *apeiron*.

That is, this second demonstration deals with a type (ii) situation, one fundamentally concerning our subject as *being displayed*.

As a final element in the comparison of the two passages and the distinction between the two results, we can note that it is logically possible for a subject to be *apeiron* only in the direct but not in the indirect sense. Every form will be provably *apeiron* in the direct sense, as it will have to have Being and Unity and so will be subject to the same regress of parts that was present in the case of The One. However, in case there are forms that do not have an infinite number of instances, these will not be *apeiron* in the indirect sense. To determine whether there are such forms goes beyond my immediate purpose, and Plato may well have thought there were not. All that matters now is that seeing that such forms would be *apeiron* in the direct but not the indirect sense may help to make clear that the two senses are importantly different. In light of this, we can observe that the two demonstrations here are not just distinguished from each other by the contrast between *to on hen* and *auto to hen* (however that is to be drawn). They also exhibit a fundamental strategic difference owing to the contrast between the two types of fact that ground predications *pros ta alla*.

Discussion of Arguments from the Text:
The Issue of Tension

We now come to our final task concerning the second section of dialectical arguments. This is to consider a sample pair of conclusions from the section that should be in tension with each other if any are, and to see whether there are any grounds here for thinking that we are to find something to reject. Because the attribution to a single subject of contradictories may be thought to be more unacceptable than that of opposites, I have chosen a pair of arguments whose joint conclusion is of the provocative, contradictory form: The One becomes and does not become younger than the others. However, since Plato treats opposites and contradictories in the same way, this pair of arguments is really quite representative of the rest of the section. Examination of this pair of passages will also be an additional occasion of confirming that the section deals with establishing results for The One *pros ta alla*, as we understand such results.

I touched briefly on a somewhat puzzling phenomenon in Plato scholarship in my remarks introducing the issues connected with the second section of Parmenides' dialectical display. Although the arguments of this section seem to me to be similar in their procedure and pattern of results to those of certain famous passages from the middle dialogues, the reaction that the *Parmenides* passages have received is different from that accorded those from the *Republic*, the *Phaedo*, and the *Symposium*.

No interpretation known to me of the middle dialogues supposes that Plato means his results concerning sensible particulars (that they are both beautiful and not beautiful, both just and unjust, both double and half, and so on) to be logically unacceptable. It is true that these results are associated with a negative response on Plato's part: they are supposed to show that sensible particulars cannot be the objects of knowledge, and are ontologically dependent on forms.

But notice that the middle-period attitude to sensible particulars, however derogatory, is so far from being tantamount to thinking the results in question violate logic that it actually depends on the logical admissibility of the results. For if this pattern of results were logically unacceptable, then far from *showing* anything about sensible particulars, it would only indicate that Plato had made some mistake in his characterization of them. And if anything is agreed on by all readers of Plato, it is that in the middle dialogues he laid great stress on his characterization of sensible particulars and the consequences he derived from that characterization. There is therefore no room for readers of the middle dialogues to suppose that Plato meant us to figure out how to *reject* the paired results that our surroundings are beautiful and not beautiful, and so on.

This means that Plato, when writing the middle dialogues, cannot have regarded all expressions of the form

A is B and A is not B

as being logically unacceptable. We might wonder whether this could mean that Plato was a contradictionist. But of course he was not. Within the *Republic* this had already become apparent, in the argument establishing distinct parts of the soul. For that argument appealed explicitly to the principle that a thing cannot be qualified by opposites in the same respect, in relation to the same thing *(kata tauton . . . pros tauton).*[12]

The key to the compatibility of this rule with Plato's characterization of sensible particulars in the middle books of the *Republic* (and in the other middle dialogues) is of course in the place holders at the end for various qualifications (''in the same respect, in relation to the same thing''). When we put all the relevant qualifications in our characterizations of sensible particulars, we get qualified formulations such as that Helen is beautiful compared with other mortals, but not compared with the immortals; Helen is beautiful physically, but perhaps not beautiful morally, and so on. Because there is no contradiction in these qualified formulations, Plato accepts them as offering no offense to logic, and rightly so.

Now, given that the qualified formulations pass Plato's logical test and he accepts those results, he is willing to accept the unqualified results as well. Since Helen is beautiful physically, Plato is willing to assert

Helen is beautiful.

Similarly, given that Helen is not beautiful morally, he accepts

Helen is not beautiful.

By joining these two results, we get one of the famous form, namely

Helen is beautiful and not beautiful.

Results of this type, so derived, are no more offensive to logic than the qualified formulations with which they are associated. This presumably also explains why it is all right for us to follow this practice in ordinary language, as we sometimes do (''We do and we don't!'').

Returning now to the *Parmenides,* I would like to show that the derivation of results in which opposites and contradictories are applied to The One in the second section of the dialectical display is of just the kind that we accept in the middle dialogues. Thus, in our sample arguments, Parmenides shows that The One becomes younger than the others in a way, and that in another way, it does not. In the qualified formulations of these results, there is no threat of logical impropriety. Because those results are accepted, he can also say that The One becomes and does not become younger than the others.

Let us turn now to Parmenides' arguments. I will not in fact quote or translate them; I think my paraphrase will be uncontroversial. One reason I paraphrase is that the text shows that The One becomes and does not become *older and younger* than the others all in one passage (stretching from 154a5 to 155c4), while for my purpose it is sufficient to trace through only the parts about becoming and not becoming *younger.* It will be obvious then how to take the same interpretative stance in regard to all the results.

Parmenides starts from the result, just established (by 153d5), that The One *is* younger than the others. From this he concludes that it is not still *becoming* younger—further time being added to the careers of two things differing in age does not affect the difference between them and, hence, does not affect their relative age. He then starts from the result (also just established, by 153b7) that The One is older than the others.[13] As additional time is added to the careers of each, the proportion by which The One's age exceeds that of the others is diminishing, so in a way The One is becoming younger relative to the others.

It is clear that the qualified formulation of this pair of results passes Plato's logical test. *In one way* (taking the absolute measure of the interval) the relative age of The One and the others remains constant, so The One cannot become younger than the others; *in another way* (considering the interval as a proportion) the relative age of The One and the others is constantly diminishing, so The One does become younger than the others.[14] The reason I selected this passage is in fact that the qualifications are beautifully explicit in the text. The summary runs:

Οὐκοῦν ᾗ μὲν οὐδὲν ἕτερον ἑτέρου πρεσβύτερον γίγεται οὐδὲ νεώτερον, κατὰ τὸ ἴσῳ ἀριθμῷ ἀλλήλων ἀεὶ διαφέρειν, οὔτε τὸ ἓν τῶν ἄλλων πρεσβύτερον γίγνοιτ' ἂν οὐδὲ νεώτερον, οὔτε τἆλλα τοῦ ἑνός· ᾗ δὲ ἄλλῳ ἀεὶ μορίῳ διαφέρειν ἀνάγκη τὰ πρότερα τῶν ὑστέρων γενόμενα καὶ τὰ ὕστερα τῶν προτέρων, ταύτῃ δὴ ἀνάγκη πρεσβύτερά τε καὶ νεώτερα ἀλλήλων γίγνεσθαι τά τε ἄλλα τοῦ ἑνὸς καὶ τὸ ἓν τῶν ἄλλων; (155b4–c4)

Inasmuch then, as one thing does not become older or younger than another, in that they always differ from each other by an equal number, The One cannot become older or younger than the others, nor the others than The One; but inasmuch as that which came into being earlier and that which came into being later must continually differ from each other by a different portion—in this point of view the others must become older and younger than The One, and The One than the others.[15]

(Compare also the remarks by which Parmenides makes the transition from the first to the second result at 154c3–6, especially *tēide . . . pēi . . . Hēi . . .* in c5–6.)

Given that in this qualified formulation there is no contradiction, Plato is right to accept the pair of results. And given this, he accepts, just as he had in the middle dialogues, the streamlined result lacking the qualifications. It is by now established that there is no more reason to discover logical impropriety here than there was in the case of those famous passages.

It should be obvious, without further discussion, that these arguments are of the kind we expect in a section devoted to establishing *pros ta alla* results for The One. I trust that discussion of these representative arguments, taken together with that of the first pair, will have made clear the way in which I take the ones I did not discuss. Having shown that we can understand the section as obtaining the kind of results I expected, and having also shown why the combined results of the section are not in unacceptable logical tension with each other, I have completed the work of this chapter. It has provided additional support for my two basic tenets, that Plato intended us to accept all the results of the dialectical exercise, and that the *pros heauto/pros ta alla* qualifications are crucially relevant to understanding the exercise.

6

On 155e4–157b5

We now come to 155e4–157b5: *Eti dē to triton legōmen* . . . ("Well, let us take up the argument yet a third time . . ."). The characterization of this passage determines whether the exercise consists in eight or in nine basic sections. (In earlier chapters, I have simply stated there are eight sections, postponing justification for that claim until now.) While seemingly pedantic, the query whether the dialectical display has really eight or nine sections is connected with larger issues. Interpretations of the *Parmenides* have the task of explaining how the sections of argument are generated, and why Plato considered the exercise so generated to be desirable. These larger stories involve commitments on the number of sections. Thus, if we can determine the correct number without appeal to any interpretative scheme, we will have evidence that can be used as a check on those larger schemes.

In particular, the Neoplatonist tradition is committed to there being nine coordinate sections.[1] This interpretation is of considerable interest, not just because of its role in the development of Neoplatonism, but also in terms of the history of the understanding of the *Parmenides*. For, as we saw in chapter 1, the Neoplatonist interpretation is alone among those developed before now in upholding all the conclusions of all the arguments. Given the problems associated with rejectionism, if the Neoplatonist interpretation were the only or the most viable interpretation avoiding rejectionism, it would be in a very strong position. The present effort of course joins the Neoplatonist tradition in seeking to show how we can accept all the results of all the arguments, though it does this in a different way. This makes it appropriate to consider which interpretation does this more successfully. The matter of the number of sections bears on this issue. The Neoplatonist scheme posits nine coordinate sections, whereas I expect only eight. Thus, if there are indeed eight basic sections, this mistake taken together with the drawbacks I explained in chapter 1 as associated with all multiple-subject interpretations will tell strongly against the Neoplatonist tradition.

Although interpreters who stand outside the Neoplatonist tradition generally agree that there are only eight coordinate sections, I do not wish to rely only on this agreement because the position (as just explained) of the Neoplatonist interpretation makes it inappropriate to decide this question against it without proper evidence. Remarks interpreters have made in support of the eight-section view (such as those of Cornford, with which I am generally in agreement) are not accompanied by as much evidence as the subject deserves. Also discussions of this point sometimes use as evidence in favor of the eight-section view some antecedently held belief about the structure of the exercise.[2] But we can only use the result of our inquiry as a check on candidate interpretative schemes if we decide the present question independently of our allegiance to our own schemes. The detailed evidence presented in this chapter should provide grounds that can be used in deciding between Neoplatonism and other interpretations, without recourse to antecedent belief about the structure of the exercise.

The number of sections in the dialectic is, for present purposes, the most important issue connected with 155e4–157b5, but it is not the only one. After this passage has been characterized, two additional ways in which interpretation of the passage bears on my investigation will require discussion. First, I will show an implication that the presence of this passage has for the strategy of Parmenides' dialectic—it has some tendency to tell further against rejectionism as the correct interpretative stance to the first two sections of argument. Second, I will have to consider a slight complication, noted by recent commentators, arising from the relation of the arguments of this passage to those of the second section. Because the understanding of the present passage to which I will be committed gives rise to the same complication, I will try to indicate ways of dealing with it.

On The Status of 155e4–157b5

In characterizing 155e4–157b5, three positions are available:

1. 155e4–157b5 constitutes a section coordinate with the other eight.
2. 155e4–157b5 is the final part of the section beginning at 142b1.

3. Although not part of the section that extends from 142b1–155e3, the lines in question do not form a section coordinate with the other eight.

The availability of this third position is important. Some interpreters believe that the passage in question is a sort of appendix to what has come before. If we can explain what role the appendix has without putting it on a par with the other sections (and especially if we can see that such an appendix would not appear on future occasions of dialectical exercise), then the view that the exercise consists essentially of eight sections will survive. For the nine-section view to be attractive, the exercise should contain *nine coordinate* sections.

Given the availability of the third position, merely determining whether our lines are part of the second section is insufficient. Finding out whether our lines form a section *coordinate with* the eight agreed-upon sections requires us not just to determine whether they have an aura of sectionhood but to determine what characterizes the eight that are agreed upon and whether this putative ninth section is *of that sort*. Thus, the proper place to begin the inquiry concerning the status of this passage is by characterizing (in a general way) all the other passages of which the gymnastic dialectic is composed.

When we compare all the agreed-upon openings of sections, we find an extremely high degree of uniformity. Some notable points are:

1. In each case the antecedent for the section (in cases I–IV "If The One is," in V–VIII "If The One is not") appears.[3]

2. Each opening after the first mentions the new inquiry in connection with whether the interlocutor wishes to consider it or whether it ought to come next.

3. In openings II, IV, VI, and VIII we find language referring to a return to the hypothesis, starting again from the beginning, and things of this sort.

When it comes to the bodies of the sections, it is common for scholars to speak as if there is a standard list of predicates whose holding or not holding must be checked out in each section. When we make up lists for the first two sections, they indeed match.

The first hypothesis considers whether The One: is many; has parts or is a whole; has beginning, middle, end; is limited; has shape (share of straight, curved); is anywhere (in itself or another); is in motion (alters, moves in place, changes place), is at rest; is same as or different from itself or another; is like or unlike itself or another; is equal or unequal to itself or another; is older than, younger than, same age as itself or another; is in time; was, has become, was becoming, will be, will become, is, becomes; is one; is the subject or possessor of anything, including name and *logos,* knowledge, perception, opinion.

The second hypothesis considers whether The One: is; is one; has parts, is a whole; is unlimited; is many; is limited; has extremities, has beginning, middle, end, shape (straight, curved, or mixed); is in itself, another; is in motion, at rest; is same as and different from itself and others; is like and unlike itself and the others; is touching and not touching itself and the others;[4] is equal, unequal to itself and the others; has a share of time; is and becomes older, younger than itself and the others; is the same age as itself, the others; was, is, will be, was becoming, becomes, will become; is the subject of knowledge, opinion, perception; has name, *logos,* and however many things belong to the others.

Sections III through VIII each discuss explicitly a much smaller number of predicates (virtually all of which are from the "canonical list"—the only possible exception is that sometimes these sections join perishing to becoming). All of these sections except V then close with a remark intended to have some general force. Section III speaks of "all the opposite affections" *(panta ta enantia pathē);* IV reads "nor has it admitted any other of the things of this sort" *(oude allo ouden peponthe tōn toioutōn);* VI says that the subject does not have "anything else of the things that are" *(allo hotioun tōn ontōn);* VII mentions "all the things of this sort" *(panta ta toiauta);* and VIII refers to "however many other things we went through in the preceding" *(alla hosa en tois prosthen diēlthomen).* The last of these phrases makes clear that it at least has in mind a list derived from previous sections. And three of the others are committed (at least implicitly) to there being such a canonical list: otherwise how are we to know what *ta toiauta* (the things of this sort) and *ta enantia pathē* (the pairs of opposite affections) could be?

We are now ready to look at the controversial section, and to see what to make of its characteristics in connection with those of the eight accepted sections. Its opening is as follows:

Ἔτι δὴ τὸ τρίτον λέγωμεν. τὸ ἓν εἰ ἔστιν οἷον διεληλύθαμεν,
ἆρ᾽ οὐκ ἀνάγκη αὐτό, ἕν τε ὂν καὶ πολλὰ καὶ μήτε ἓν μήτε πολλὰ

καὶ μετέχον χρόνου, ὅτι μὲν ἔστιν ἕν, οὐσίας μετέχειν ποτέ, ὅτι
δ᾽ οὐκ ἔστι, μή μετέχειν αὖ ποτε οὐσίας;

Well, let us take up the argument yet a third time: If The One is such
as we have said, musn't it—being one and many and neither one nor
many and having a share of time—have a share at some time of Being,
since it is one, and since it is not one, at some time not have a share
of Being?

The first two clauses of this opening contain the two main pieces of
evidence for setting up the opening with what follows as a genuine
section. The phrase *"Eti dē to triton legōmen"* tells us clearly that we
are doing something for the third time. In fact, if we were trying to
divide the arguments into sections without help from centuries of
scholarship, and so did not use the agreement of previous editors and
commentators as a guide, one of the most obvious starting points for
us would be this opening, since it clearly tells us that something that
has already been done twice is now to take place for the third time.

The most straightforward way of taking this is to suppose that, since
this introduction is followed by six other clear beginnings, we have
here the third of nine sections of equal standing. However, nothing in
the text rules out a slightly more involved interpretation that takes the
"to triton" to refer to a third effort at getting conclusions concerning
The One, but rather as an auxiliary inquiry than as one of the main
sections. Although the straightforward is *prima facie* preferable to the
involved, it will be well to keep both in mind and to decide later
which of these two interpretations deals best with all the evidence.

The second piece of evidence for the sectionhood of our passage is
the second clause; this passage starts off from an antecedent of its
own: *to hen ei estin hoion dielēluthamen* ("If The One is such as we
have said"). This, like the first piece of evidence, suggests that our
passage is not just part of the second section. But, like the first piece
of evidence again, this does not tell us whether to take our passage as
an auxiliary inquiry or as one of the main sections. So while these two
pieces of evidence allow us to rule out the second of our three options
(taking the passage as the final part of the second section), it does not
decide between the remaining two. To do that, we need to find out
whether this passage is a section of the same sort as the other eight.

We have already touched on two of the three shared features of
openings in connection with our passage. It displays the first feature

at a general level, since it contains an antecedent. However, attention
is due to an important difference between the present antecedent and
those of the other eight openings. All of the other eight were from the
pair

>   If the One is

>   If The One is not

announced in the methodological remarks as the starting point for the
exercise. However, the present antecedent is not one of these two, but
is rather:

>   If The One is such as we have said.

We can appreciate more fully the deviation this brings from the
other cases when we understand the force of "such as we have said"
(hoion dielēluthamen). For

>   If The One is such as we have said

is not merely an indirect way of saying

>   If The One is

or

>   If The One is not.

Rather, the arguments in this passage rely on The One's having been
shown to have (at least some of) the canonical predicates and their
contradictories (and/or opposites). So this passage differs importantly
from the others in starting from results already obtained.

The third feature is one that the present section in a way overshoots.
(This feature was in any case not shared by *all* the new openings.) For
while openings II, IV, VI, and VIII speak of starting again or something of that sort, the present lines are much more particular, giving
an actual running count, as I mentioned before.

We may finish with the opening by noting that the second feature
of the other openings is not present here. The absence of an explicit
discussion and agreement concerning what comes next has some tendency to suggest that what is to come involves less of a new departure
than the other sections do.

We now come to the body of the section. A glance through 155e4–

157b5 shows that this passage certainly does not follow the pattern of determining whether the canonical predicates hold or fail to hold of some subject. This is not surprising if it is true that the antecedent for this section is that The One is such as to have the canonical predicates and their contradictories (and/or opposites). What we find instead is a discussion of becoming and perishing (here added to becoming for the first time in the dialogue), and points connected with them and the notion of change. Given the close-to-complete matching of the predicates used in the other sections, the circumstance that nothing from the list appears here is clearly significant.

We may summarize our results now by noting that none of the three features of the relevant openings is precisely displayed here, and that the all-but-universal correspondence in the bodies of the sections is wholly absent in this case. These circumstances clearly outweigh the preferability of giving a straightforward interpretation of the phrase *Eti dē to triton legōmen* ("Well, let us take up the argument yet a third time"); their recognition puts us in a position to say that the lines in question constitute a section, but not a section coordinate with the other eight. That is, we have determined that the third of the three possible answers to the question of the status of the section is the correct one.

What, then, should we make of this passage? Given its characterization as starting from (at least some of) the results that have already been established and then going on to point out consequences in the domain of becoming, perishing, and change, we would like to know the answers to two questions:

1. Why does such a section appear at all?
2. Why is there not such a section whenever the generation of systematically contradictory (or opposed) results would seem to warrant it?

The first question can be broken down further into two questions: why does Plato include these results, and why does he not include them in the second section of arguments? The first subquestion can be answered easily: the results are of importance and interest, and ultimately allow the derivation of conclusions for The One that display the pattern of thoroughgoing surface paradox that Plato so clearly found attractive. (An indication of the interest of Plato's work here in historical context is the great influence of arguments from the *Parmenides* concerning becoming, time, and change on Aristotle's *Physics*, to which

G. E. L. Owen drew attention in *"Tithenai ta phainomena"* and "Aristotle on Time." Notice that the group of arguments Owen calls "too important to omit"[5] is the group from our present passage.)

As for the separation of this inquiry from the second section proper, a superficial reason for it is the departure of the section from investigation of the applicability of the canonical predicates. Less superficially, we can speculate that recognition that the topic of the moment of change needed work prompted Plato to segregate the essay. Progress here is not, in the first instance, about The One. But such progress was a necessary precondition to deriving certain kinds of results for The One in relation to the others. And the essay on the moment of change involves material whose novelty and difficulty make it hard for it to be placed easily in the second section proper.

I think that the answer to the second question is a special case of something clearly true of the dialogue: that the arguments of successive sections get shorter because they are able to presuppose what has already been established. We do not need a section "like the present one" whenever an appropriate antecedent becomes available because such sections would not differ enough from what we already have to be worth writing down. Having already provided the arguments that show what conclusions about becoming, perishing, and change follow for anything that is "such as we have said," Plato relies on us to realize that they can be applied again at various points in the succeeding arguments. Casual introductions of some particular results (for which we presumably should supply these arguments) occur at 160a5, 162b9–c6, 163a7–b6, 163d1–8, and 165d7.

For similar reasons, we should not expect the production of passages corresponding to this one on subsequent occasions of dialectical exercise. On those occasions it will be possible to apply the analysis of change achieved in this passage as easily as it is applied in the subsequent sections of argument here. Thus there will be no need for a section additional to the basic eight in future.

We have now supplemented our claim that the passage in question is not a section coordinate with the other eight with some positive suggestions about the passage: we have explained why it appears, why Plato does not include this material in the second section proper, and that we should not expect a section like the present one on future occasions of dialectical exercise. This completes the demonstration that the dialectical exercise consists essentially of eight sections.

Further Evidence Against Rejectionism

In chapter 1, I presented a series of general reasons against adopting "rejectionism" as our response to the gymnastic dialectic that forms the second part of the *Parmenides*. We are now in a position to appreciate an indirect way in which the particular passage that is our present subject bears on the issue. (I label as "rejectionism" the approach that takes the ostensible results to be interpreted to be so unacceptable as to constitute a signal to reject something that led to those results. I pointed out in my earlier discussion that, since contradictions are unacceptable, the belief that the dialectic's results are genuinely contradictory leads naturally to rejectionism, whereas the belief that the contradictions are merely apparent is independent of rejectionism.)

The production of the present passage has some tendency to tell against rejectionism as applied to what came before, this tendency being greater or lesser depending on what the grounds for the rejectionism are and which exactly of the results derived so far serve as starting points for the present passage.

It might be tedious and more than the point is worth to set this issue out in greatest detail. The basic point is just that the deriving of further results from what has come before makes little sense on the rejectionist view of what has come before. According to rejectionism, we have already seen that we have derived unacceptable results, and plan to find things to reject so as to set things right again later. Before we have done that, it has little point to derive further results from a group we have identified as problematic. If our starting points are themselves unacceptable, this will infect the results we derive from them. Even if our starting points should turn out to be an acceptable subset of the problematic group, we are not yet in a position to know that. (Parmenides and Aristotle have not made any utterances indicating what we can save and what sacrifice.) It is thus too early to go on to derive further results with propriety *on the rejectionist view* of what has come before. Yet Plato's production of the section indicates that he thought its results were worth deriving. This provides further evidence against rejectionism.

A Complication

We come now to the final issue of this chapter, consideration of a certain problem involving the bearing of 155e4–157b5 on the interpretation of the preceding section of dialectical argument. The problem, which has already been identified by other commentators, arises for my interpretation as well. In fact, thorough treatment of this issue belongs to the study of Plato's views on the moment of change, a topic far removed from the theme of this book. I include this discussion not because I feel sure about any response to the problem, but rather because it seems, on the one hand, necessary to face the difficulty and, on the other, hopeful that several responses to it are in fact available. The problem can be stated in two different ways, and each formulation suggests a possible response. I shall consider both in turn.

One way of putting the problem is as follows. My interpretation of the second section proper stressed that the conclusions of that section were not in fact in tension with each other. Although the streamlined conclusions predicated opposites and contradictories of The One, these were associated with formulations introducing qualifications that prevented real contradiction. (We thus had The One becoming younger than the others *in a way,* and not becoming younger *in another way.*) We did not investigate in detail the range of qualifications that applies here, but in fact there is a varied range. In particular, the qualifications are *not* confined to the introduction of time indices—the example I just mentioned (and discussed in chapter 5) shows that. Indeed, this is what we should have expected, on the basis of the *Republic,* where the example (at 436d4–e6) of a top spinning in place and so both moving and at rest is not presented in terms of time indices. That is, the top is not said to be in motion and at rest at different times, but in different respects. Similarly with the familiar example of Helen's beauty. We commonly think of Helen being beautiful in one context (compared with other mortals) and not beautiful in another (compared with the gods). Seemingly, this need not involve any insistence on Helen's being beautiful and not beautiful at different times.

However 155e4–157b5 seems to be going on the assumption that when we have a result of the form

The One is P and not P

we can immediately conclude that the qualified formulation that avoids contradiction is one involving time indices. This appears immediately in the first inference of the passage, that if The One is to be one and many and not one and not many, it must be one and not one and therefore have a share and not have a share of Being *at different times*.

Cornford and more recently Mitchell Miller also stress in their interpretations of the second section proper the compatibility of that section's results (without need for the addition of temporal qualifications). Realizing the difficulty this creates in using those results as starting points for the present passage, they propose "regenerating" (Miller's term)[6] results that would require the introduction of time indices. This is especially easy for any interpreters who may be accustomed to importing a newly defined subject at the beginning of each section. However, I believe this is a practice to be avoided. But we can resolve the difficulty without having to produce results not part of what "we have said."

Specifically, we could pay attention to an implicit temporal dimension in the process of division that, in the beginning of the second section of arguments, took us from The One (which was one at the start) and divided it into its Unity and Being, and so on, making it indefinitely multitudinous. It is, possibly, proper to say that before division The One is one and not many, and after division it is many and not one. This would involve taking the division seriously as an occurrence with a location in time, instead of thinking of it as an atemporal conceptual analysis of The One.

Whether or not this is desirable, it is obvious that the other paired results do not lend themselves to this treatment, since they are not all obtained by the description of processes that we can choose to locate temporally. Therefore to carry on with this line, one would have to stress a difference between the way in which The One's being one and not one come into our present passage, and the way in which the other incompatible pairs are introduced. We have in the text:

τὸ ἓν εἰ ἔστιν οἷον διεληλύθαμεν, . . . ὅτι μὲν ἔστιν ἕν, . . . ὅτι δ' οὐκ ἔστι . . . (155e4 ff.)

If The One is such as we have said . . . since it is one . . . and since it is not one . . .

But later, when the other pairs are introduced, we see not "since" with the indicative, but "whenever" with the subjunctive, as, for example, in 156c1–2:

Ὅταν δὲ κινούμενόν τε ἵστηται καὶ ὅταν ἑστὸς ἐπὶ τὸ κινεῖσθαι μεταβάλλῃ . . .

Whenever, being in motion, it comes to a stop, and whenever, being stationary, it makes the change to moving . . .

(The formulations of which this is representative start at 156b6.)

Possibly this distinction is due to Plato's awareness that only The One's being one and not one have been established by the second section proper in the sense in which the present passage requires. He introduces the other pairs hypothetically so as to free investigation of the moment of change from being restricted to results the second section has established.

The other way of putting what I think is fundamentally the same problem is to use the distinction T. Irwin developed between what he in "Plato's Heracleiteanism" styled "*a*-change" and "*s*-change." For our purposes, we can skip the formal definitions and start from Irwin's statement that

> The intuitive difference between *s*-change and *a*-change is that in *s*-change the changing object is being compared with itself at some previous time, and the reference to different times is essential to the explanation of its different properties. *a*-change, like *s*-change, involves the presence of opposite properties in different situations, but the reference to different times is not needed to describe the different situations, and the changing object is not compared with itself at a previous time. We can speak temporally of *a*-change, and say that food is sometimes healthy and sometimes unhealthy; but we can equally explain the different properties nontemporally, by reference to the different consumers of the food.[7]

Part of Irwin's purpose is to say that though Plato does not distinguish explicitly between *a*-change and *s*-change, we need not conclude that he conflated them illicitly, either. But our passage raises the worry that such an illicit conflation occurs, after all. For, in Irwin's terms, in the second section proper Plato demonstrated that The One undergoes *a*-change. (Hence the marked presence, on describing the results, of *hēi men . . . hēi de . . .*, rather than *tote men . . . tote de*

. . . , which would have been suited to descriptions of *s*-change.) Yet, strangely, the passage 155e4–157b5 suddenly acts as if we are dealing with *s*-change (saying that The One can only be one and not one if it is each at a *different time*).

One possible conclusion is that Plato, alas, did conflate the two. Another is to exploit the hint that it is not impossible to treat *a*-change as keyed to time elements: the time one context is active, and the time another is. This would allow the results of the second section of arguments to introduce the analysis of the moment of change legitimately. Although time-indexed *a*-changes are not typical of all changes in time (since *s*-changes have at least as much of a claim to be central, and are presumably more important from the point of view of physics), this does not prevent them from being adequate to introduce analysis of the notion of change in time. For clearly nothing in the analysis depends on the particular character of the individual changes that introduce the discussion. It relies only on features common to all cases (including *s*-changes) of change in time. Thus, insofar as the purpose of the passage is to make progress with the analysis of the moment of change, it does achieve that (and presumably has obtained results that can be applied later to cases of *s*-change as well). Insofar as the purpose of the passage is to make possible the derivation of further results for The One, by connecting the results of the second section with this investigation of change, it does that too, if the adaptation of *a*-change so that it is keyed to times is reasonable.

Conclusion

I would like to leave discussion of this passage here, since I think it has gone far enough for my purposes. (Further understanding of the passage is desirable, but will be part of the investigation of Plato on change, rather than of study of the structure and purpose of the gymnastic dialectic.) Whatever the correct positions on the elements of interpretation of the passage we have not settled are, we have established that

    (a) the passage is an auxiliary inquiry rather than a main section

    (b) the passage's presence has some tendency to tell against rejectionism

(c) the passage's line of argument is not irreconcilable with interpretation of the second section proper as having results that are consistent as they stand.

Thus, my interpretation of the dialectic as consisting in eight main sections of arguments, all of whose conclusions are to be accepted, continues to be confirmed.

7

The Third and Fourth Sections
of Argument

This chapter concerns the third and fourth sections of Parmenides' dialectical display. As we progress through these and the later sections, my treatments are getting shorter. This is common to all interpretations (except those that do not treat all the sections explicitly). An obvious reason for this is the length of the sections: whereas the second section was over thirteen Stephanus pages in length, the last six are all under three pages (and two actually take up less than one Stephanus page each). So in a very superficial sense, these later sections contain less evidence. Moreover, a fairly substantial picture of what is going on will have emerged by the time one comes to these later sections, and one may already have mined important nuggets of information from them.

Thus, I used the evidence of the openings and closings of all the sections to confirm my determination of the structure of the exercise in chapter 2; I also relied heavily on significant passages from the fifth section to determine the force of the *pros ta alla* qualification, in chapter 3. Since this evidence was used at the beginning of the inquiry, we have now only to deal with what is left. All these factors join together to determine the role of the coming treatment of the later sections. It will not introduce wholly new elements to the basic interpretative framework. Rather, given the framework and the text's receptivity to being interpreted in accordance with it, we will be reading off and interpreting each section's results and thereby getting new information about The One and its role in the world (according to Plato).

What then do we expect to find going on in the third and fourth sections of gymnastic dialectic? Our study of the structure of the exercise tells us that these two sections should find out what follows for the others, if The One is, and that one should be devoted to results for the others *pros heauta,* and the other to results *pros to allo.*[1] Indeed, if the ordering of the general description of the exercise is to be followed exactly, the third section should give the results *pros heauta,* and the fourth those *pros to allo.* However we noted in chapter 2 that there was some minor variation between the general and particular descriptions of the exercise, when it came to the orderings of the sections. Nevertheless, the following two things remained constant in all cases. The overall grouping was always that all the results from a positive hypothesis came first, followed by those from its corresponding negative hypothesis. Also, the qualifications used to describe the sections were the same in all the descriptions: each section was described by a combination of one each from the following three pairs: *if the positive hypothesis obtains / if the negative one does, what follows for the subject / for the others,* and *in relation to itself / in relation to the others.*

Since the first two sections of Parmenides' gymnastic display have derived results from a positive hypothesis (if The One is) for The One in relation to itself and in relation to the others, we can confidently expect that the third and fourth sections will complete the investigation starting from the positive hypothesis, one section deriving results for the others *pros heauta,* and one section deriving results for the others *pros to allo.* But we need not be so dogmatic about the order in which the sections should do this. The ordering with results for the others *pros heauta* first and then results for them *pros to allo* should probably be thought of as an arrangement to be observed in general, but which can be altered in particular cases for particular reasons.

Indeed I have already noted, on the basis of the section openings (in chapter 2, in confirming my understanding of the exercise's structure) that the third and fourth sections do derive results for the others, if The One is. What we will find out in the body of this chapter is that the third section derives results for the others *pros to allo* (i.e., in this case, *pros to hen*), whereas the fourth finds results for the others *pros heauta.* In fact, there is considerable agreement already on what is going on in the third section. (There is a basic account common to the treatments of Cornford, Sayre, and Allen).[2] And as is to be expected with all sections *pros ta alla,* my account will not differ much from these.

One very useful contribution of these three scholars is to have pointed out how part of this section is connected with the longer treatment of the *apeiron* in the *Philebus,* and how both texts can be understood in accordance with Aristotle's reports on Plato's metaphysics.[3] For our section's study of the others as they are in fact shows that they can be thought of as resulting from the interaction of two principles: there is a theoretically isolable, indefinite stuff, which becomes limited and articulated by The One. In effect, we get a glimpse in the *Parmenides* of the elusive Indefinite Dyad. Since it is impossible to pursue this within the present work, I will confine myself to explaining the passage in connection with my theme of the structure of the dialectical exercise and the bearing of the in-relation-to qualifications on it.

Thus, I will explain what the third section is doing in terms of its *pros to allo* mission. This will ultimately lead to the observation of a special connection between the investigation of the others *pros to allo* and *pros heauta,* in this case. This will be a connection between the two sections that does not hold in general. Rather, the fact that it holds in this case will be a significant manifestation of the special role The One has in the world as a principle. This connection between the sections will be exactly the sort of special consideration that justifies minor modifications in the general ordering of the sections. Thus, we will be able to see a good reason for the departure from the general ordering of the sections.

The dependence of the results for the others *pros heauta* on the results *pros to allo* will in fact be so strong that the results of the fourth section will be explained virtually instantly after that. All that will then remain in the fourth section to be discussed is the summary with which it closes. I will therefore close this chapter by explaining the reasons for adopting Heindorf's conjecture for the lines that close the fourth section, and thereby the first half of the dialectical exercise (160b2–3). This explanation will be fulfilling a commitment made earlier, since I adopted Heindorf's conjecture for purposes of my discussion in chapter 3, but postponed discussion of the matter until we came to its place in the text.

The Third Section Characterized

I noted that the third section of arguments derives results for the others *pros to hen,* if The One is. We now need to look at the justification for that claim. The first main result of the section so obviously is engaged in a project of this kind that it does not require much discussion. For the record, I take the line of argument of 157c3–e5 to be as follows. The group, the others, since it is *others* (rather than *other*) has parts.[4] Parts are parts of a whole, so the others are a whole. Being a whole involves displaying Unity, so the others display Unity—that is, they are one *pros to allo*. The passage 157e5 ff. then shows that each part of the whole must also have a share of Unity, again in an uncontroversial way. Construing this passage in the standard way amounts to taking it, in the terms of my scheme, as deriving results for the others *pros to allo*. This suggests that we take the section as a whole as a *pros to allo* section.

Certainly, if the section is intended to derive results for the others *pros to hen,* if The One is, it is not surprising that the section's first result should be that the others taken as a group and also individually exhibit Unity. Indeed, someone might mistakenly think that this is all that we should find in a section so characterized: what else about the others' exhibiting Unity is there to investigate? Before we consider the next passage in detail, it may help to describe briefly its basic project.

Parmenides, in 158b5 ff., taking it as established that the others do display Unity, proceeds to analyze the situation further. He abstracts their displaying Unity from the others, and sees what this leaves. That is, he starts with the others as they are in fact, each one displaying Unity, and then engages in the conceptual project of removing their Unity from the others. At this point someone might say, "What an elaborate way of going about things! And after all, it produces nothing different than the original others." In seeing why this is not so, we will see a manifestation of The One's role as a principle.

By contrast, one can imagine starting with a class of philosophy students. Everyone in the class is in fact a student, but we can imagine abstracting this and imagining each one with the feature Studenthood removed. This still leaves them as fairly robust individuals. The important thing about The One is that the corresponding claim is not true: when we imagine taking their Unity away from the others we are not left with the same group only changed slightly; we rather find them totally undone and no longer capable of being identified as individuals at all. When considering these two cases, we can readily say that their display of Unity is much more vital to the others than their display of Studenthood is to the members of a class. Thus, although our passage's project of abstraction is in a sense considering the others independent of their exhibiting Unity, it does so in a way designed precisely to discover how important their relation to The One is to them: it allows us to observe (by comparing the situations before and after the abstraction) what difference their displaying of Unity makes to the others.

Now we can identify the tasks that remain in connection with the third section of Parmenides' display. The first is to understand what is involved in the basic project of abstraction. The second is to appreciate how the result of the present abstraction differs from corresponding results when the exercise is done with other subjects. In a sense, we can distinguish two aspects of the result of this passage. Under its first aspect, the result is typical of what we would imagine in the corresponding case on any other occasion of gymnastic dialectic: it contributes to the analysis of the others' displaying the subject. But under its second aspect the result is highly unusual. The bearing of the abstraction project on the availability of truths about the others *pros heauta* will be due, ultimately, to the fact that The One is so important that nothing else can be coherently distinguished without it. Let us now turn to our tasks.

The Project of Abstraction

Our first task is to understand the basic project of abstraction. Since I have announced that this abstraction is part of the project of seeing the importance of their relation to Unity for the others, readers may be surprised by the language Plato uses at 158c5–6, 158d5–6, and 158e2. The occurrences of *kath' heauta/ēn* (taken by themselves / itself) and *phusis* (nature) may be thought to suggest that the others are being taken *pros heauta* after all. But here as always, it is not enough simply to note that certain language occurs; we need to determine *how Plato is using it*. It will turn out that *phusis* here does not mean nature in the narrow technical sense on which I have been concentrating; rather it is used in an ordinary way. (cf. Plato's use of *eidos:* he clearly feels free to continue with ordinary uses of words, even those he uses for vital technical purposes.) [5]

Let us consider how a certain project that could be described as considering something taken by itself can be a part of inquiry *pros to*

allo. An everyday example analyzed by common sense displays a similar structure to the case we have in the text. Suppose that, in a discussion of shark's fin soup, someone asks what shark's fin is actually
like and receives the reply that it is valued for its texture, but that its
flavor in the soup is wholly derived from that of the other ingredients,
as shark's fin *in itself* (or by itself, or taken by itself) has no flavor.
This is not equivalent to saying:

Its account includes being flavorless.

Nor is it equivalent to:

It is no part of its account that it be flavorful.

Although this second claim is at least true, it still does not have the
right force. To see this, we need only observe that the whole point of
the assertion is to distinguish shark's fin from, say, abalone, but that
the claim

It is no part of its account that it be flavorful

applies equally to both. The account of abalone will presumably clas-
sify it according to genus and species or genetic structure; this is at
least what the commonsense background we are imagining for the conversation would attribute to it. Similarly, the commonsense view of
the account of shark's fin (if it has one) would presumably be along
the lines of viewing it as a certain part of a shark, whose account is
to be given in terms of genus and species or genetic structure. Thus,
neither being flavorless nor being flavorful will be part of the account
of sharks or their fins.

Given that the two candidates

Its account includes being flavorless

It is no part of its account that it be flavorful

have not succeeded in glossing the present use of

In itself, it is flavorless,

we need some way of taking ''in itself'' and ''taken by itself'' that
does not suggest that it offers an account of the thing. Clearly the idea
is that of abstracting something from a combination in which we have
been considering it as forming a part. Thus in the shark's fin case, we

are interested in it as something that is to figure in a soup, but we want to discuss what its flavor would be *were it not* combined with the other ingredients, where this flavor (or absence of flavor) is part of what qualifies it to be so combined. Notice that, on trying a bit of shark's fin from the soup one could legitimately say

This is very flavorful

because it takes on flavor in the soup, by its relation with the other ingredients.

There are always disanalogies between commonsense examples and the philosophical cases with which they are meant to help us. Nonetheless, this example does indicate that such phrases as "in itself" and "taken by itself" may be used, in a context where some compound or complex is being discussed, to isolate a subject for discussion that is one of the elements to be combined, but will now be considered in abstraction from the combination.[6] The crucial point is that, though we are discussing the element as abstracted from the compound under discussion, this is not yet necessarily to be focusing on its account: we are interested in characteristics that make it suitable for figuring in the combination whether or not they are named in the account.

Next we can observe that corresponding to this ordinary sense of taking something by itself, there is an ordinary conception of nature: we determine something's nature by considering how the thing is or would be on its own (as opposed to how it is perhaps made to be by outside influences). Thus our expression "a natural blonde" gets its sense from contrast with "a peroxide blonde"—that is, one whose blondeness "comes out of a bottle."

We are now ready to return to our passage. The language with which it begins shows that the others are still being discussed as participants in The One. Indeed, 158b5–7 refers to them repeatedly under that designation, rather than with the more usual "the others." So the wording stresses strongly that the others are participants in The One. Strikingly, these very participants are said to exhibit indefinite multitude rather than unity.

The lines that follow explain how this can be. They are:

ἄλλο τι οὐχ ἓν ὄντα οὐδὲ μετέχοντα τοῦ ἑνὸς τότε, ὅτε μεταλαμβάνει αὐτοῦ, μεταλαμβάνει; (158b8–9)

When they are coming to have a share of Unity, they aren't then one
nor do they have a share of Unity, do they?

These lines make it clear that what I and other commentators have
been calling a procedure of abstraction is in view. Taking it as established that the others do participate in The One, they want to consider
them at a stage conceptually prior to that participation.

Parmenides then (at 158c1 ff.) points out that, if we consider the
others in this way, having abstracted from them their participation in
The One, the others are multitudes among which there is no Unity.
On their own (i.e., taken apart from The One) the others are wholly
without limit and so they run together into an indefinite mess. To
consider the others in this way is to consider them taken by themselves
in the sense I have been explaining; and it is to investigate their nature
understood as: what they do not owe to their relationship to something
other than themselves. This context thus provides occasion for the ordinary uses of *kath' heauta* and *phusis*. That is, as I take it, the language at 158c5–6, 158d5–6, and 158e2 has the force: taken on their
own (i.e., in isolation from their relation to The One) the others are
wholly indefinite and unlimited. We should not insist on seeing the
text's language as setting up an inquiry that is designed to obtain results for the others *pros heauta*. Rather, the procedure of this passage
is well construed as being part of a response to the theme question:
what follows for the others in relation to The One, if The One is? Just
as shark's fin, considered in the context of a discussion of soup (rather
than of its scientific account), can be truly said to be flavorless (which
makes it suitable to be combined) and to be flavorful (once it has
benefited from being combined), so the others considered *pros to hen*
can be said to be not one, but unlimited in multitude (which is suitable
at a stage conceptually prior to participation) and to be one (once they
have benefited in participation).

Our discussion has made explicit that what turns out for the others
pros to hen is not confined to the truth that the others have a share of
The One. The circumstance that all truths to do with their exhibiting
Unity come under this heading involves inquiry into what the others
must be prior to exhibiting Unity. Thus we have a subdivision of the
results for the others *pros to hen* that corresponds to (without mirror-
ing exactly) the subdivision of the results for The One *pros ta alla*.
For one way of describing the results of the second section of gym-

nastic dialectic is to say that examinations of The One both as display-ing and as suitable for being displayed appear there, all under the general heading: what follows for The One *pros ta alla*. Similarly, we have here examinations of the others both as displaying Unity and as suitable for doing so under the heading: what follows for the others *pros to hen*.

The Bearing of the Third Section on the Fourth

We have now seen that the basic procedure of examining what the others must be like at a stage conceptually prior to their participation in the subject need not automatically lead to results concerning their accounts. Thus, whereas we expect these elements to be present in any section deriving results for others *pros* a subject, we will not ex-pect such sections generally to bear on the study of those others *pros heauta*. However, although the framework of the exercise does not guarantee it, it turns out that the special role of The One as a principle of everything will manifest itself in there being such implications in this case.

We are now ready to examine the special way in which, in our text, the section considering the others *pros to allo* will bear on the section considering them *pros heauta*. The best way to appreciate the unusual character of this implication of our passage is to compare our text with what can be expected on other occasions of doing the dialectical ex-ercise. If the subject of an exercise were, for example, Motion, then we would expect, corresponding to the third section of the present exercise, a section investigating: if Motion is, what follows for the others in relation to Motion? If we project what this section would be like on the basis of the understanding of Parmenidean dialectic we have been developing, we will expect its basic results to emerge from consideration of the two conceptual stages of the others' displaying of Motion. That is, we would expect to see two topics treated: what is true of the others in virtue of their display of Motion, and what is true of these others if we take away their displaying of Motion? This ap-proach would lead to two basic results. First, that the others move. Second, that the others do not move (but perhaps have some features that amount to being capable or receptive of Motion).

These results have superficial similarity to those of the third section of arguments in the text, but there are also deep differences. For a start, in the *Parmenides* it not only turns out that the others are one, but just *being others* actually requires participation in The One. This is what the argument to the conclusion that the others are one depends on; yet no such reasoning is going to be what establishes the corresponding result about Motion: the others than Motion will not have to move just to be others than Motion.

Let us now turn to the second of the two basic results that we projected for the others than Motion: the others do not move. We can see that it is superficially parallel to the corresponding result in the *Parmenides:* the others are not one, but rather are indefinite in multitude. However, there is a crucially important difference between the two results, deriving from the importance of what the others lack once they are deprived of display of the subject. Although being motionless may have some further implications concerning features that the others cannot have if they are taken in abstraction from their Motion, these consequences will be limited. That is, when the subject is Motion, we can imagine that the others, considered in isolation from their display of Motion, might turn out to lack Locomotion (since it is a kind of Motion) but to require parts (in case parts are needed if the others are to be suitable to participate in Motion). It will be true of these others *kath' heauta* (i.e., in abstraction from their display of Motion) that they are motionless and have parts.

However, there is no reason to suppose that the abstraction from their display of Motion tells us anything about the accounts of those others. That is, it has no bearing on what holds of them *pros heauta.* In particular, being taken in abstraction from Motion does not destroy the status of the others as determinate individual forms each associated with a determinate individual nature. Therefore, this deprivation will not be so thoroughgoing as to prevent them from being proper objects of study *pros heauta.* Thus, this section will not have any particular consequences for the section whose theme question is: if Motion is, what follows for the others in relation to themselves?

Yet, the third section of our dialectical display does have implications for the *pros heauta* section. Parmenides starts out considering the others in abstraction from their display of Unity (which is to consider them *kath' heauta* in only the modest sense I developed earlier)—that is, he is plainly doing something understandable as part of an inquiry concerning the others *pros to hen*. But as we just saw, when they are taken in isolation from The One, the others run together into an indeterminate mess: indeed, it is only from their combination with The One that the others get limit with respect to each other (158d3–5). Once they have run together to this extent, it will no longer be possible to identify determinate natures (in my technical sense) among them to be articulated by accounts—that is, truths *pros heauta*. Or, to put it another way, since the others considered in isolation from their display of Unity become indeterminate, there will not be any substantive truths that hold of them, and *a fortiori* none that hold of them in virtue of themselves. This brings us to the special relation between the third and fourth sections of arguments in the *Parmenides*: the results of the third section in fact imply that *there can be no positive results* in the fourth. That is, considering the others *pros to hen* shows us that their display of Unity plays such a crucial role for the others that trying to think of them in isolation from this cannot succeed.

If there is to be such a relation between the two sections, the fourth section's study of what results for the others *pros heauta* must be required to take them in isolation from their relation to The One, since The One is not one of the others. Indeed, Parmenides' exhortation to engage repeatedly in gymnastic dialectic makes more sense if this fourth section is to discuss what natures remain to the others once their display of the subject is abstracted, for two reasons. First, we can see that doing this is a way of getting information about our subject's role in the world. Second, if the project were to get results for the others *pros heauta* without bothering with the abstraction, then a single demonstration of the fourth section would preempt all the first sections of all the other exercises. Parmenides would not then be reasonable in recommending them all as needing to be done.

If the results for the others *pros heauta* are indeed to deal with post- (rather than pre-) abstraction others, then, since the third section has shown us that the others, in abstraction from their relation to The One, collapse utterly into an indeterminate mess, the third section already has shown us a general reason owing to which the fourth section will not have any positive results. In having this relationship, the third and fourth sections of the present dialogue differ from analogous sections with different subjects. This explains the observed ordering of the sections—given the direction of the implication, the third section is needed to prepare us for the fourth. This consideration is clearly sufficient to outweigh the presumption that sections *pros heauta* should precede the corresponding sections *pros to allo*. Besides, whatever intuitive reason there is to discuss things *pros heauto* before they are discussed *pros ta alla* will always be counterbalanced by a certain convenience that comes from having the two *pros ta alla* sections occurring side by side.

The Fourth Section of Arguments

We have seen that the third section of arguments has shown that, if the others are taken in abstraction from The One, they are in no shape to have positive natures. Therefore, if an inquiry *pros heauta* must take them in abstraction from The One, then as the fourth section opens we already know a good reason for which it can have no positive results. Let us now see if the text is compatible with this reasoning's being applied.

The passage 159d1–4 tells us that the others have no share of The One, that they are in no way one, and that they do not have any one among them. In this situation we can apply the moral of the third section. The passage 159e2–160b1 can be read straightforwardly as relying on this. The general idea here is:

If the others were certain things, they would have a share of a certain number, the number of things they were.

But having a share of any number requires having a share of The One.

That's been ruled out.

So the others are not anything.

On Heindorf's Conjecture

The fourth section of arguments concludes with a sentence summarizing the conclusions obtained so far, or at least the sentence does this if we accept Heindorf's conjecture. Without the conjecture, the sentence reads:

Οὕτω δὴ ἓν εἰ ἔστιν, πάντα τέ ἐστι τὸ ἓν καὶ οὐδὲ ἕν ἐστι καὶ
πρὸς ἑαυτὸ καὶ πρὸς τὰ ἄλλα ὡσαύτως. (160b2–3)

Thus if The One is, The One is all things and not even one in relation
to itself and in the same way in relation to the others.

If we consider how inapposite such a summary is at the end of the
fourth section, it is surprising that both Burnet and Diès seem to ap-
prove it (Diès does not even print Heindorf's conjecture in his apparatus). Cornford gives the conjecture in a note, but does not discuss
the issue.

What makes the summary as it stands inapposite is that it clearly
refers only to what results for The One—that is, it gives the results of
the first two sections of argument only. On the other hand, what it is
natural for a summary to do (and what all the others of the many
summaries that appear in the *Parmenides* do) is to include mention of
the most recent results: a short summary may give only the developments of the immediate context, whereas a longer one may start further back in leading up to the recent results.

The fuller formulation suggested by Heindorf, however, refers sche-
matically to the results of each of the four sections we have had so
far. It reads:

Οὕτω δὴ ἓν εἰ ἔστιν, πάντα τέ ἐστι τὸ ἓν καὶ οὐδὲ ἕν ἐστι καὶ
πρὸς ἑαυτὸ καὶ πρὸς τἆλλα, καὶ τἆλλα ὡσαύτως.

Thus if The One is, The One is all things and not even one in relation
to itself and in relation to the others, and the same is true of the others.

The second *talla* here gives the desired reference to the third and fourth
sections. Comparison with the final summary of the dialogue as a whole
tends to confirm the conjecture. A summary at the end of the sections
starting from the positive antecedent *ei hen esti* ought to include one
half of what the summary of the dialogue as a whole does. In fact
the final summary is remarkably similar to the sentence as emended.
It is:

ἓν εἴτ' ἔστιν εἴτε μὴ ἔστιν, αὐτό τε καὶ τἆλλα καὶ πρὸς αὐτὰ καὶ
πρὸς ἄλληλα πάντα πάντως ἐστί τε καὶ οὐκ ἔστι καὶ φαίνεταί
τε καὶ οὐ φαίνεται. (166c3–5)

Whether The One is or is not, it and the others in relation to themselves and in relation to each other are all things in all ways and are not, and seem and seem not.

As I stated in chapter 3, whether or not we accept the emendation, the summary with which the fourth section closes uses the phrase *kai pros heauto kai pros talla* and so it provides evidence for my claim that the *pros heauto* and *pros ta alla* qualifications bear importantly on the exercise. If the emendation is to be accepted, we can take the sentence as summarizing the results in the most economical fashion possible: it gives us the combinations of devices that have been used so far (we have used both members of the *pros heauto/pros ta alla* pair, and derived results both for The One and for the others, but we have used only the positive hypothesis) and then gives the four general conclusions that both The One and the others are everything and nothing.

8

The Results from the Negative Hypothesis

In the present chapter I will complete the project of showing how Parmenides' demonstration works as an instance of the new exercise as I understand it. We will now consider the four sections of argument devoted to deriving consequences from the negative hypothesis: if The One is not. These sections are themselves brief and can be dealt with succinctly. Their brevity and their results in fact support certain ideas I had begun to develop earlier. As we will see, the extremely elliptical form of some of the arguments here is strong inducement to accept the notion that later sections are relying on the results of earlier ones. The other main idea that will receive support concerns not the procedure of the exercise but its import: the results from the negative hypothesis complete the introduction of The One as a principle, that is, something without which nothing else can even be thought of, and which is itself not to be understood in terms of other things.[1]

To understand these final four sections as carrying out gymnastic dialectic is of course to see how each section is rightly characterized as deriving results either *pros heauto* or *pros ta alla*. It also requires seeing how the individual sections have their place in the ordering of the exercise as a whole. In one case, there will be a departure from the ordering of sections generally recommended, which will need special explanation. We will also make progress on a less schematic point: the argumentation of the sixth section will provide a hint about the special association between natures and forms, which will be useful later for the project of reconstructing the way in which Plato wished to think about forms.

The Fifth Section of Gymnastic Dialectic

Given what we know from Parmenides' methodological remarks about the general scheme for generating and ordering sections, we might expect that the first section of results from the negative hypothesis would find out what results for the subject *pros heauto,* and the next one would inquire into *pros ta alla* results for the subject. In fact, on the present occasion this expected order is reversed. I will now briefly explain why I take the first set of results from the negative hypothesis to be *pros ta alla,* and then speculate on what special consideration could have prompted its present position.

My own preceding treatment of certain arguments[2] from the section already established it as an inquiry *pros ta alla;* these were key pieces of evidence in my original development of the force of the *pros* qual- ifications. Another consideration that confirms this derives from com- paring the results of this section with those of the first section of ar- guments. That section found, on the supposition that The One is, that all predicates failed to hold of The One *pros heauto.* Now a glance at the fifth section of arguments shows that its overall result is that the predicates considered do hold of The One. It would certainly be very strange if The One had gotten into a position to have all these predi- cates hold of it *pros heauto* just by being supposed not to be. Rather we should take the pattern of results to indicate that this fifth section is indeed *pros ta alla,* and that the sixth (which will deny all predi- cates to The One) will take up the task of finding out what follows for the subject *pros heauto.*

Let us turn briefly to the issue of whether the way of understanding the section suggested by these large-scale motivations indeed makes sense of its contents. The arguments are in fact straightforwardly con- strued along the lines developed for understanding inquiry *pros ta alla;* none invites construal as *pros heauto.* Since the matter is too clear to require extended discussion, while the arguments are too varied to be given a single schematic treatment, I will simply take the opening lines of the section (160b6–e2) for illustrative purposes.

The starting intuition of this passage is that the hypothesis ''If The One is not'' is different from another possible hypothesis. This brings on a general claim that begins to analyze what lies behind this. Var- ious statements presumed to be different are so because it is plain they speak of different things that are not—that is, we know they have different subjects. So too in the case of our present hypothesis: our sense of it derives from its subject being known, and being different from certain others. That is, when someone says "If The One is not," it is plain that what he speaks of is different from the others, and we know what he is talking about. Thus there is knowledge of The One, and it has Difference.

Clearly this discussion works[3] if it is trying to show that The One is known and different *pros ta alla*. Notice however that it could not even be thought to show that being known and being different are part of being one. That is, its strategy of starting from our sense of the negative hypothesis as different from other possible hypotheses is not at all suited to inquiry *pros heauto*.

We must now consider the issue of the placement of this section. It has clearly gotten ahead of the place the general ordering for dialectical exercise assigns to inquiry *pros ta alla*. What we need to discover is why this should be so. It seems to me that a reason for this placement is not hard to find. Given the attack on Not-Being put forward by the present speaker's namesake, the historical Parmenides, the viability of hypotheses of the form "X is not" should not be taken as uncontroversial. Some exploration of the circumstance that we in fact can understand such assertions and distinguish their various subjects from each other is apposite as a counterpoise to Eleatic proclamations about the blank unmanageability of what is not. The opening of the section as we have it (that is, the passage I just treated) in fact takes up this issue. It seems, however, that such a topic would not be very happily placed at the beginning of a section that achieves no positive results, since that could then appear to be an indication of the hopelessness of getting anywhere from a negative antecedent. (Cf. the reaction of many interpreters to the negative results of the first hypothesis.) Since the section of results for The One *pros heauto,* if The One is not, is a section that achieves no positive results, Plato could have felt it was better not to inaugurate the program of deriving results from his negative hpyothesis with it.

The Sixth Section

We come now to the sixth section of arguments, prepared with the expectation that it examines what results for The One *pros heauto,* if The One is not. We have already identified one reason for the lack of

positive results in this section: The One had no *pros heauto* predicates
when it was supposed to be, and being supposed not to be could not
make any predications of the proper sort obtain. However, the present
section will have its foundation in a consideration that does not trade
on the special status of The One (163c2–d1). This consideration will
then make possible an argument to show, even of a subject that has
pros heauto predicates if it is, that if the subject is not, then no predicates hold of it *pros heauto*. The reason for including this passage
when the section could be finished in much shorter compass may be
to prepare us for future occasions. After all, the *Parmenides* is explicitly intended to start us off on a series of dialectical exercises, taking
in turn a series of different subjects. And it will in general not be true
that subjects have no *pros heauto* predicates, if they are.

The foundation for this section is the claim that statements of the
form "X is not" signify the complete absence of *ousia* of whatever
they declare not to be (163c2–3). It is easy to read the text of the
section as building on this claim in inquiry *pros heauto*. To do this,
we need only take the absence of *ousia* as comprehending the absence
of the associated nature. The passage 163e6 ff. will then clearly note
the very general implications of the absence of The One's nature. If
we keep in mind that *pros heauto* predication is grounded in relations
between natures, it is apparent that if The One has no nature it has no
pros heauto predicates: for a nature that is not can appear in no tree,
and so a *fortiori* can appear in no tree below another nature.

To read the passage in this way we need to take the *ousia* on whose
absence it trades as the One's nature. Linguistically this is no problem;
nature is always a leader among possible glosses for the word. Notice
however that the claim that whatever is not has no *ousia* may seem
suspect when we become aware of taking it as including the claim that
whatever is not has no nature. Someone might think that claim vulnerable to the counterexample that Humanity is, while Socrates is not.

There will in fact be some profit for us in reflecting on the force of
the claim in question for Plato. In any case it is an interpretative re-
sponsibility to work out why he took it to be true. We noted earlier
that it might be only forms, and not sensible individuals, that are each
specially associated with a unique nature. (The idea was that Humanity is just one of many natures, Musicality, Paleness, and so on, which
all have some relation to Socrates, but no one of which is specially
his nature.) This would eliminate the counterexample I introduced:

Humanity now does not count as Socrates' nature, so its surviving him is irrelevant to the claim. Still, for Plato to take the claim that whatever (form) is not has no nature to be acceptable, he must have thought there was no counterexample available in which a nature has a career independently of the associated form. That is, he must have taken forms and natures to be so closely associated that when some form is taken away, the associated nature cannot remain. We can consider later how we might conceive of this association more particularly (whether, for example, natures can be taken to be components of forms).

The Seventh Section

Given the lessons of the third and fourth sections of argument (roughly, that thinking about the others in abstraction from the fact that they have a share of The One cannot get anywhere), we expect negative results from both of the remaining sections. And indeed both the seventh and eighth sections do have basically negative results (the seventh manages the customary appearance of contradiction with its successor only by introducing the consideration of seeming). Thus to determine which character we should assign each of them, we need to consult the arguments they contain.

The seventh section can in fact be identified as *pros ta alla* on the basis of the following:

Οὐκοῦν καὶ ὅμοιά τε καὶ ἀνόμοια δόξει εἶναι;—Πῇ δή;—Οἷον ἐσκιαγραφημένα ἀποστάντι μὲν ἓν πάντα φαινόμενα ταὐτὸν φαίνεσθαι πεπονθέναι καὶ ὅμοια εἶναι. (165c6–8)

Then won't they appear both like and unlike?—How?—As with scene paintings, to the distant spectator all appearing to be one will appear to have suffered the same and so to be like.

These lines take everything's seeming to be one as counting as everything's seeming to have suffered the same, and so seeming to be like. This follows if we read the assertions as *pros ta alla*. However, if we try to take the passage as dealing in *pros heauto* predications, it does not yield a good argument. Waiving for the moment doubts about whether The One has species, two things A and B would give the appearance of being one *pros heauto* if their natures seemed to be

below One in a correct tree of kinds. Clearly this would give no grounds
for the conclusion that A and B give the appearance of being like *pros
heauto*—for that they would have to appear to be below Like. And
since we already know One is not itself below Like, seeming to be
below One would do nothing to establish this result.

The seventh section, therefore, gives results for the others *pros to
hen*, if The One is not. Let us now briefly note what emerges from
the section as a whole. To start it may be worth observing that there
is a certain tension in the very project of the section. For as we learned
in the third section, the others are dependent on The One even to be
others, or to have any determinate quality. Thus supposing, as the
section does, that, although The One is not, we may yet speak of "the
others" is somewhat problematic. The text at 164b6–7 indicates that
Plato here starts from the assumption that we can in fact talk about
the others. That is, so to speak, he grants himself that to get things
going. We then find (as we could have guessed from the results of
previous sections) that if The One is not, the others are not one or
definitely numerous. But, in addition, the approach of seeing what
follows from the supposition that we can speak of others leads in a
new direction: we get results concerning what the others seem; notably
they seem to form unities (164d7), and this puts them into a position
to seem to have other properties. To appreciate the significance of this,
we might contrast, for example, Cat and consider the question: what
follows for the others *pros* Cat, if Cat is not? We will not expect any
such conclusion as that they appear to be cats. It is a rather special
fact about The One that, even when it is hypothesized to be absent,
the others will *seem* to be related to it. This is a further manifestation
of The One's status as a principle.

The Eighth Section

Finally we come to the last section, which we expect will give what
results for the others *pros heauta*, if The One is not. Given what we
have already learned about the dependence of the others on The One,
the negative character of this section is overdetermined. That is, we
know there are no positive *pros heauto* truths concerning the others
than The One even on the supposition that The One is; and the present
section demands that we start from the supposition that The One is

not. We may note a parallel in language between this section and section four, which marks their shared strategy. In section four, at 159d1–e1, Parmenides pointed out that the others were in no way one and had no one among them, and therefore that they could not be any definite number either. This then made possible the conclusion that no positive predicates could apply to the others *pros heauto*. Our present section has (corresponding to 159d1–e1) the remarks at 165e4–166b3. Whereas the results of the fourth section were due to the others being considered in isolation from The One, the results in the present case follow from the circumstance that The One is supposed not to be. The circumstance that there is no one among them makes the others of the present section eligible for the same reasoning applied in the fourth: they cannot be many in any definite way, so they can have no distinct natures. The immediacy with which the conclusions of this section follow the remark that the others are not nor do they seem to be one or many is striking. The text moves right on to:

Οὐδ' ἄρα ὅμοια οὐδὲ ἀνόμοια.—Οὐ γάρ.—Οὐδὲ μὴν . . . (166b3–4)

Nor are they like nor unlike.—No.—Nor . . .

That is, we get an extremely plain list of results, without any reasons or explanations. This strongly supports the supposition that the basic reasoning is that already developed: that when they are taken in isolation from their relation to The One, the others collapse.

My basic project, of interpreting the second half of the *Parmenides*, is now complete. We can judge how far we have come by reconsidering Plato's own concluding statement:

Εἰρήσθω τοίνυν τοῦτό τε καὶ ὅτι, ὡς ἔοικεν, ἓν εἴτ' ἔστιν εἴτε μὴ ἔστιν, αὐτό τε καὶ τἆλλα καὶ πρὸς αὑτὰ καὶ πρὸς ἄλληλα πάντα πάντως ἐστί τε καὶ οὐκ ἔστι καὶ φαίνεταί τε καὶ οὐ φαίνεται.

Let this be said therefore, and that, as it appears, if The One is or is not, it and the others in relation to themselves and in relation to each other are all things in all ways and are not, and seem and seem not.

This passage, at first glance so full of paradox, now stands as a most accurate summary of a successful exercise, and we now, perhaps for the first time, can attach their full significance to all the phrases Plato employs in this summary.

In the course of chapters 3 through 8 we have seen how, when read with the addition of the in-relation-to qualifications, the conclusions of the various sections of arguments are not in any real contradiction with each other. We have also seen that, when the conclusions are so read, the arguments given to establish them are good ones. In fact, the attempt to construe the arguments sympathetically in light of the methodological remarks turned out to require the development of the *pros heauto/pros ta alla* distinction. This gives the distinction some claim on being considered Plato's key new innovation. In order to determine how far it is suited to that role, we will need to consider whether it has any use in connection with the problems of the first part of the dialogue. For after all, Plato introduced the new exercise precisely to give help with those problems. Thus returning to consider the problems now is, as I said in chapter 1, to put our main results in their natural context. That will be the task of the next chapter.

9

The Resolutions of
the Difficulties

Now that we have come to a satisfactory understanding of the second part of the *Parmenides,* we are in a position to consider the question of the relation between the two parts of the dialogue. In chapter 1, I conceded that we could not take Parmenides' remarks as guaranteeing that the dialectical exercise would yield solutions to the famous problems of the immature Socrates—the exercise could be merely preparatory. Nevertheless it seems indisputable that if the developments of the second part of the dialogue do provide a response to the problems, that is the response that will have been Plato's. Thus the purpose of the present chapter is to assess whether the exercise in which we have been engaging gives us resources relevant to the famous difficulties. But before turning to detailed consideration of the particular arguments, let us consider the situation in a general way.

The views of the Socrates of the first part of the dialogue have always reminded readers of certain passages from the great middle-period masterpieces, perhaps especially the *Republic* and the *Phaedo.* For convenience, I will call the position produced by concretizing the suggestions of those passages in the most simpleminded way " 'Platonism.' " The purpose of the scare quotes is of course to mark the fact that I question whether Plato himself had any enduring commitment to this position. There is however no doubt that many people have thought that he did.

Intuitively, the most bizarre feature of "Platonism" was that it thought of Beauty as the single most beautiful thing, of Largeness as doing its job by outclassing all other objects in size, and so on. That is, "Platonism" was supposed to be a view that, for one thing, believed in entities that managed impossible feats of superinstantiation.[1] Moreover, the functional role of these entities was that of properties. Beauty, say, was supposed to be somehow the common thing among a group of sensible beautiful individuals. (This is of course why the forms have a series of names of the form "Beauty," "Justice," "Largeness," as well as "The Beautiful," "The Just," and "The Large.") Thus, as an anachronistic reader might put it, "Platonism" makes the ridiculous mistake of thinking that properties do their job by having the very properties they are. The superexemplification theory of forms seems obviously to be a mistake.

Let us now see how our investigation of the *pros heauto/pros ta alla* distinction is connected with all this. Clearly, the superexemplification view results naturally in taking sentences of the form

   The Just is just

to be doing the same kind of thing, or describing the same kind of state of affairs, as those like

   Aristides is just.

That is, to reintroduce now the terminology of the professional secondary literature and of my own investigation, the superexemplification view assimilates the crucial self-predication sentences to everyday true predications *pros ta alla*.

In chapter 1, when discussing the situation of the immature Socrates, I developed the thought that ideally Plato should both recognize that self-predication sentences may be trivially false on one reading, and also find another reading on which they are true. The *pros heauto/ pros ta alla* distinction can now be seen to be designed to enable him to do exactly that. For example,

   The Just is just *pros ta alla*

will be trivially false. For if being just is having a soul in which each part does its own (as the *Republic* held), or indeed is any condition on persons or their behavior, then The Just will not be the kind of thing that could be just *pros ta alla*—that is, that could display the feature in question. Nevertheless,

   The Just is just

can still be true when it is made as a predication *pros heauto*. The fact that a single form of words can change its truth value depending on whether it is being used to make a predication *pros heauto* or *pros ta alla* is of course one of the very basic characteristics of the distinction to which Parmenides' dialectical exercise has accustomed us. It is also clear that, when they are made as predications *pros heauto*, self-predication sentences will always be true. It was the failure of the immature Socrates to recognize that the *pros heauto* reading was to be pursued that led him as I put it to misinterpret his own theory. Let us now proceed to take up the particular arguments in which Socrates revealed his incompetence, in order to see how someone who has exercised properly may avoid trouble.

Good-bye to the Third Man

Perhaps the notoriety of the Third Man Argument is a reason for starting our discussion with it. Certainly the straightforward way in which the *pros heauto/pros ta alla* distinction applies to it is one.

> Large things must have some one thing in common (sc. The
> Large)

is in itself not problematic; Plato can continue to analyze this in terms of the large things being related to a single form, The Large. We noted before that, while the argument is seriously underspecified, it relies on some version of the crucial claim

> The Large is large

in order to reach the threatening conclusion

> The Large and the other large things now require something new
> in common, by which all of them will appear large

Indeed, the production of new Larges depends crucially not just on the claim that The Large itself is large being made, but on that claim's being treated in the same way that (say)

> Montblanc is large

would be. To begin with, The Large itself and the original group of visible large things are treated as being large *in the same way*. This induces the notion that we have a new group of large things whose display of a common feature must now be analyzed in the same way the display of the common feature of the original group was. If this is taken to require the introduction of a new form, a regress is started. And the regress will be vicious, given the purpose of forms. Each form purports to be the single thing that grounds and explains the predications it is invoked in connection with and should therefore not yield to an unending series of further forms.

But now that we have exercised, we can see immediately that there are two different predications the single form of words

The Large is large

could be used to make. It is important to Plato to maintain the *pros heauto* predication. But we are now clear that that predication does not claim that The Large itself is large in the same way that the original group of large things is. It therefore does not force on us a new group of large things whose display of a common feature requires us to crank up our machinery again and produce a new form.

The example of Man may make this even clearer.

Man is man

and

Man has vertebrae

are ridiculous if we read them as being the same sort of assertion as

Socrates has vertebrae.

However,

Man has vertebrae

does express a truth that conveys part of the structure of the world, namely that having vertebrae is part of what it is to be a man. Because he takes them to express the real structure of the world, it will always be important to Plato to maintain the predications *pros heauto*. But the crucial point is to realize that he now has an interpretation of these important sentences on which they make no claims about the forms' exhibiting features. The *Parmenides* has now emerged as showing conclusively that Plato does not suppose each property to do its job by having the property that it is. Because his support of the self-predication sentence does not require him to take The Man itself as an additional member of the group that displays the feature common to men, and as requiring a new form to explain the display of this new group, there will be no regress. Plato's metaphysics can say good-bye to the Third Man.

The Whole/Part Issue

Let us now consider whether participants get the whole or a part of a form in which they participate. It is worth noting that while the elenctic purpose of his encounter with Socrates causes Parmenides to concentrate on the problems associated with each of these choices, there is also a significant motivation realized in each. The immature Socrates got into trouble with each of the two alternatives, which he considered to exhaust the possibilities and to be mutually exclusive. We can in fact cater for both motivations while avoiding trouble—so that each alternative will be maintained in a way.

The motivation for saying each participant gets the whole of a form is as follows. A fundamental reason for having forms is to give some real content to the claim that certain individuals have something in common. This is most clearly achieved if there is a single thing to which all the relevant participants are related in the same way, suggesting that perhaps the whole form should be related to each participant and not distinct parts of the form to distinct participants.

To get a feeling for the thought that each sensible composite should get only a part of a form as its share, let us take an Anaxagorean example. Suppose a certain ring and a certain bowl both to be golden. If we now take The Gold to be the totality of (pure) gold in the world, we can say that the ring and the bowl are each golden in virtue of their having shares of The Gold. In this example we clearly want to say that the share each gets is a *part* of The Gold, and certainly not the whole. To put it another way, the ring accounts for only part of the being of The Gold.

Let us now consider how someone who has exercised can treat each option (attempting to preserve what is good in it without falling into Socrates' difficulties). The first option considered in the text is that each participant gets the whole of the form. The motivation in favor of this is now honored by positing, in each case in which several individuals display a common feature, a single nature to which they all conform. For example, if being just is having a soul in which each part does its own, then this is explanatory of all just things (not some part of it of one, another part of it of another). The worry associated with this alternative was supposed to be that if the whole of the form is in each of several individuals that are separate from each other, the form would be separate from itself. Since the mere fact that we invoke the whole nature in understanding the participants is no reason to consider the whole form to be *in* each individual, this worry has been outgrown.

Let us go on now to the option that each participant gets a proper part of the form. The *Sophist* is well known to analyze, for example,

Theaetetus is sitting

to indicate that Sitting has being in relation to Theaetetus. (263a2 ff.) Thus Theaetetus and I each account for part of the being of Sitting, but of course precisely not by having discrete physical parts of it as ingredients in our bodies. This will be the survival in Plato's view of the Anaxagorean apportioning of parts of forms to participants.

It is more to the purpose now to consider whether Plato has outgrown the problems connected with this option. In the first part of the dialogue, Parmenides did not content himself with presenting a single distressing consequence of the claim. Rather, he started by pointing out that it makes the forms divisible, and then said (first) that they were in that case not one, and then (at great length) derived further absurdities from the dividing of the forms. Let us consider each of these attacks in turn.

The mere fact that something is divisible or even has separable or actually separate parts does not automatically mean it cannot be one thing. The new scheme has the resources to claim that the form is not in the position of (say) a ragbag whose contents have been scattered throughout the world. Nothing continues to associate the various scraps once they are scattered. However, the parts of the being of a form represented by disparate participants are associated: they bear the marks of their conformity with the single related nature.

Let us now turn to the (much lengthier) second type of objection Parmenides makes to having the forms be divisible. He presents problems in handling the cases of The Large, The Equal, and The Small, but we can continue to use The Large as a representative case (as I did in chapter 1). The problem was supposed to be that it is unreasonable to divide up The Large, give a participant one of these parts, and then claim that the participant is large because of this part, which is *smaller than* The Large itself. In order to understand why this was supposed to be problematic, I supplied the thought that Socrates was thinking of participation in an Anaxagorean way: he was thinking that when something acquires a property, the property is transferred to the participant by coming with its share of a form *that itself has the property*. In the case of The Large, we saw that Socrates would approach the situation by remarking that The Large is large, and that other things can become large by getting a share of it. The difficult part then was that the general scheme required him to say these shares that things would get would make those things large by bringing their largeness with them. Socrates did not know how to make this claim for them, once it had been pointed out that they are smaller than The Large itself. The fact that something is small seemed to him to rule out any claim that it could be responsible for bringing largeness.

Here as in the case of the Third Man, the key to the situation is the rejection of the superexemplification view of forms. This makes it clear to us now that we should not suppose that properties are transferred to participants by coming with shares of forms that themselves have the property. Instead, we will now say

The Large is large *pros heauto*

and

Other things become large *pros ta alla* by their relation to it.

Most important, we will precisely *not* give any role here to

The Large is large *pros ta alla*.

A fortiori, the fact that an individual's share of the form is a small share—that is, is small *pros ta alla*—is no kind of threat.

The "Greatest Difficulty"

The "greatest difficulty" now appears to be no difficulty at all; it is like the Third Man in admitting a straightforward application of the *pros heauto*/*pros ta alla* distinction. As I pointed out in chapter 1, the difficulty takes its starting point from the conjunction of the claim that since forms are *kath'heauta* they cannot be in us, with the observation that forms associated with relations have their being in relation to other forms and not in relation to the things around us, whereas the things around us are related to other things around us and not to the forms.

The easiest way to consider the difficulty is to return to the particular version of it I developed using the case of Arithmetic. In this case, the claim about the pattern of relations yielded

> Arithmetic knows The Numbers (and presumably not anything around us)

and

> The knowledge of this world knows numerous collections of objects around us (and presumably not The Numbers).

Then, since this world's knowledge did not know The Numbers, and since we were obviously not Arithmetic itself, nor could we have it in us, it followed that:

> We do not know The Numbers.

A fortiori we could not be in a position to apply knowledge of The Numbers in order to derive our knowledge of numerous collections of objects around us. Moreover, by the claim about the pattern of relations, there could in principle be no such application of Arithmetic. For by that claim, only we and the things around us, not Arithmetic, could be related to sensible objects.

Let us proceed by collecting the responses that the gymnastic dialectic has enabled us to make to some of the statements that are crucial in generating this result. Now is a good time to admit that

> Arithmetic knows The Numbers

formerly had always a strange ring; we felt unsure what it meant, perhaps a little embarrassed by it, and were accustomed to peoples' hurrying it by with the thought that it is the sort of thing Plato presumably did believe. Now we have an interpretation on which it can be asserted unproblematically, for we can say without embarrassment

> Arithmetic knows The Numbers *pros heauto*

and

> It is not the case that Arithmetic knows the things around us *pros heauto*.

Further, we can certainly say

> It is not the case that our knowledge knows The Numbers *pros heauto*

and

> It is not the case that we know The Numbers *pros heauto*.

Plato would regard the first two of these four *pros heauto* statements as being true in virtue of the fact that the correct account of Arithmetic is that it is knowledge of The Numbers and not anything in terms of things around us (in this sense Plato is indeed a Platonist). And the last pair of assertions also holds: we and our knowledge are too particular to figure in the accounts grounding truths *pros heauto*.

We now come to the crucial point. As must be very familiar, none of this gives us grounds for rejecting the ordinary truth:

> We know The Numbers.

This last is of course true as a predication *pros ta alla,* and the *pros heauto* claims we accept are not at all incompatible with it. Thus the crucial inference that the difficulty needs to make at this point (to: we do not know The Numbers) cannot now be made. Further, we can now see that the mere fact that Arithmetic has its *ousia* in relation to The Numbers is no reason for thinking that it can have no application to the sensible world. Of course accounts of natures are in terms of other natures; but this has no tendency to show that the structures of those natures may not be explanatory of any particulars that indeed exhibit them.

In chapter 1, I wrote that the stress in setting up this problem on the claim that the forms have their *ousia* only in relation to *(pros)* other forms, whereas we are what we are only in relation to other sensible particulars, indicated that it would bear on the problem if it became clear that there is a way in which sensible particulars are what they are in relation to the forms. I trust it is evident that this has happened. Forms do have their *ousia* in relation to forms—the nature of Siblinghood is not given in terms of us. And we are of course the siblings of each other and not of The Sibling Itself. But when we now consider more closely this claim that we are siblings of each other, we have become able readily to pronounce that Plato will regard it as a true predication *pros ta alla*. That means the most fully specified way of putting it is:

   We are siblings of each other *pros* The Sibling.

Thus, it can be true both that we are siblings of each other and not of the form, and that we are what we are in relation to the form. As chapter 3 has shown us, the relation in question to the form is simply not the sibling relation. This is ultimately why the form is not competing with our blood relatives: each has a distinct role of its own.

   To generalize, Plato holds that we and the things around us do not figure in truths *pros heauto*. Equally he recognizes that many relations are like the sibling relation in relating sensible particulars only to other sensible particulars. We now see that he can maintain all this and still assert coherently that there is a way in which sensible particulars are what they are in relation to forms—now that he is clear about the distinct relations that ground predications *pros heauto* and *pros ta alla*.

Conclusion

We can now record answers to some of the issues raised in chapter 1 concerning the problems of the first part of the *Parmenides*. The fundamental question was that of Plato's attitude: did he know how to respond to the difficulties and if so what course did he propose? A related issue developed after study of the individual arguments. For we saw that Plato's presentation of the difficulties by itself enabled us to say neither that they all admitted a common treatment nor that each one arose independently. Chapter 1 proposed that we should expect to answer these questions only after study of the second part of the dialogue.

   On the question of Plato's attitude, I pointed out that if the gymnastic dialectic does contain advances relevant to the difficulties, we should take their application to be Plato's response to the problems. I trust it has by now become clear both that the exercise does have coherent positive results and that their application to the problems of the immature Socrates is fairly straightforward.

On the lesser point of whether the problems admit a common treatment, I think that they do. Without wanting to get bogged down in false issues over exactly how to individuate mistakes, I think it is fair to say this: simply by employing the *pros heauto/pros ta alla* distinction, we resolved the Third Man, the Greatest Difficulty, and the lengthy second of the two objections to the "part" alternative from the Whole/Part discussion. The difficulties associated with the "whole" alternative and the first objection to the "part" option were overcome by the use of materials available to anyone with even a sketch of the sort of metaphysical picture one needs to develop in connection with understanding the *pros heauto/pros ta alla* distinction. Thus there is a meaningful sense in which achieving understanding of the distinction enables an aspiring Platonist to handle the difficulties of the first part of the dialogue.

10

Epilogue

My project of understanding the key advance of the second part of the *Parmenides* has already received its basic application: we have seen that the notorious difficulties of the first part of the dialogue are no threat for Platonists who have made the advance. However, some issues that I raised in the course of my exposition still need to be considered, a process that will lead naturally to reflection on the philosophical importance for Plato's development of the crucial episode on which we have been concentrating.

Before discussing the individual difficulties with which Parmenides confronted Socrates in the first part of the dialogue, I produced a list of problem areas that interpreters generally recognized Socrates as having. We should now consider the question of what has become of these problems. Of course, it is true that since a Socrates equipped with the *pros heauto/pros ta alla* distinction will no longer fall into the difficulties Parmenides posed, the list of problem areas no longer needs attention *lest we fall into those difficulties*. Nevertheless, it is desirable to return to consider the list: it did specify important respects in which the immature Socrates fell short, and it is of interest to see now to what extent the exercise of the *Parmenides* may have led to progress. In fact, problem areas (4) through (7) have already been taken care of in the course of chapter 9. So what we have to consider now are (1) through (3): the issues of the extent of forms, of what participation is, and of what sort of things forms are.

The issue of the extent of forms required no argument to demonstrate Socrates' perplexity: he admitted it. Because there is no argument, there is really nothing specific we can now attempt to sort out, but the following speculation may not be wholly out of place. Perhaps Soc-

rates' reluctance to accept forms of man, fire, and water and his re-
vulsion from those of hair, mud, and clay are due to the influence of
some sort of superexemplification picture. For of course, he wants his
forms to be glorious entities and would naturally feel this to be incompatible with being muddy. Yet the superexemplification view must take
the form, Mud, to be some supremely muddy thing.[1] We could then
take Parmenides' remark that Socrates will come to accept forms of
all these things (and Plato's own positing in the *Philebus* [15a4–5] of
the forms Man and Ox) as indicating rejection of the superexemplification view.

The second problem I identified was Socrates' lacking a definite, viable understanding of participation. And I have mentioned repeatedly
that we had come upon something the immature Socrates would take
to be participation, but cautioned against our using that notion since it
was not yet understood. Let us now take the opportunity to attempt
some reconstruction. Of course we now reject outright Socrates' original suggestions that participation is having a physical share, or is
resemblance. Indeed, it seems that the tendency of the *Parmenides* is
to recommend abandoning any monolithic notion of participation. This
will at least be true if Plato wishes to continue invoking participation
in the range of cases he has been accustomed to do, that is, if he
regards all true subject-predicate assertions as being ultimately grounded
in participations.

For most obviously, Plato has been accustomed to saying, for example, that Aristides is just because he *participates in* Justice. But he
also says such things as that Justice participates in Virtue.[2] In fact,
both usages occur in the second part of the *Parmenides*.[3] This indicates that Plato retained the word "participation" and did want to
continue invoking it in the full range of cases. After all the work we
have been doing to study predication *pros heauto* and *pros ta alla* and
the relations grounding them, we see immediately that in the first kind
of case, participation amounts to the relation grounding predication
pros ta alla, and in the second to that grounding assertion *pros heauto*.
It may initially seem a disadvantage that we now are introducing a
rather more complicated notion of participation; on the other hand, the
treating of two importantly different relations as if they were one—
participation conceived monolithically—formerly created a great deal
of trouble.

We can also get information from the *Parmenides* on the traditional question whether forms can participate in other forms, or whether the condition of participant is reserved for sensible particulars. We now know that forms will not only participate in other forms, but will do so in both ways (at least most forms, those that are not principles, will do so). For example, The Cat participates in The Animal in one way, and in The One in the other; that is, it is *a species of* Animal, and it *displays* Unity. We will explore the implications of this rich pattern of participations in the course of the next section, when we turn directly to forms.

The third problem area for the immature Socrates was his incompatible and unacceptable ideas about the sort of things forms are. We noted before that these views were related to his views on participation; we will see that the *Parmenides* seems to be recommending notions about forms whose increased complexity answers to that in the version of participation we have been discussing. Here too, I think the loss in simplicity, while no recommendation in itself, was acceptable to Plato since he realized that a simple notion of forms as something like superexemplifiers was untenable. In fact, to construct a ''New Theory of Forms'' is beyond the scope of the present work: I see the *Parmenides* as inaugurating rather than preempting the program of the late dialogues. So what I will say now about forms purposely holds back from being a description of a complete theory Plato held dogmatically. What I will do is try to pull together the indications that can be gleaned from my study of the *Parmenides,* in order to see what suggestions and constraints we can find for new thinking on forms.

One very obvious fact about the scheme we have found introduced in the *Parmenides* is that it gives a central role to *natures*. Thus there is an issue about what the status of these natures is to be. One clue from chapter 8, which can be stated very briefly, is that there must be a connection between forms and natures so close that a nature cannot remain when the associated form is taken away. A straightforward way of ensuring this would be to take natures to be in some way components of forms. Reflection on the lessons of the *Parmenides* taken by itself does not reveal, at least to me, whether Plato in fact meant to take this, or some other option. I hope that future study, perhaps of the *Philebus,* will provide further guidance on this issue.

The new development in thinking about forms that emerges most strongly from my study is of course that they must be such as to have two kinds of truths about them: those *pros heauto* and those *pros ta alla*. It will in fact serve to expand our viewpoint if we now consider some implications of this basic fact. Let us start by taking some examples. When we consider Justice *pros heauto*, we will be giving an account of what it is to be just; when we turn to consider it *pros ta alla* we will find that it is one (one form) and many (a whole of many conceptual parts) and so on. The results of our own dialogue have already shown us that when we consider results for The One *pros ta alla* we find that it also is both one and many; we can easily anticipate that The Many too is both one and many *pros ta alla*. That is (to make a point which was raised preliminarily in chapter 5) we can now observe a marked change in Plato's pattern of assertions. For in the middle dialogues, their figuring as subject terms in truths of the form

A is B and A is not B

seemed to be characteristic of sensible particulars—and in virtue of this they were said to "roll around between being and not being"; forms on the other hand were whatever they were purely and without qualification, that is, in such a way as not to bear the opposites or contradictories of their predicates.

The circumstance that sensible particulars rolled about between being and not being while forms did not was, in the *Republic*, the basis of the metaphysical and epistemic priority of forms. What both is and is not was derived from and dependent on what is. (This view is echoed in the first part of the *Parmenides*, at 128e6 ff.) And the ontological categories were paralleled by the types of cognition. Knowledge was said to be set over what is, and opinion over what is and is not. Thus forms only could be objects of knowledge, whereas sensible particulars were the objects of opinion. There even seemed to be some difference in the appeal to us of the two kinds of things: in the *Symposium*, its immunity from rolling about seemed to be the source of the superior attraction of The Beautiful as compared with all other beautiful things. In general the prominence of this distinction between forms and sensible particulars in the middle dialogues is familiar.[4] It is thus no small thing for Plato now to produce results according to which forms roll around too—and the *Parmenides* is designed so as to highlight such results: its second section of gymnastic dialectic and the projected second sections of all such exercises consist solely in results of the rolling-around type. As the examples we have considered show, these are not necessarily restricted to being of the form

    The F is G and The F is not G

but can even include some of the form

    The F is F and The F is not F.

Let us consider now the philosophical significance of this new pattern of assertions.

We can see Plato as having an enduring interest in marking off a certain class of privileged truths, because of his belief that what is really F and cannot be not F is prior to what is both F and not F. Clearly, since sensible particulars do not in general display their features in a stable, pure, and unconfused way, observations on their displays cannot amount to the privileged truths in question. If we make the assumption that there are some extra individuals that are not sensible and that have the desired properties without their contradictories, we get a picture that indeed yields the hoped-for class of privileged truths. The privileged class is simply the class of truths about these fancy new individuals. However, the wish to deny that these special individuals bear predicates opposite or contradictory to their eponymous ones—for example, that The Many can be one—creates problems very quickly. It comes into conflict with the thought that if The Many is going to be *a* form it will have to be one, and with the idea that since the forms should be stable and tranquil, Motion, like the others, ought to be at rest; it seems easy to think of more such problems. In fact, to believe in special individuals of this kind is to be what I called in chapter 9 a " 'Platonist.' " And we have seen from our study of the first part of the dialogue how aware Plato was of the dangers of that.

   If Plato saw that a distinction between forms and sensible particulars based on their pattern of displaying features was not viable, could he develop another method of marking off his class of privileged truths? Our study of the *Parmenides* shows that he did: the privileged truths are the truths *pros heauto*. These indeed articulate structures that are explanatory of the world. And clearly, this class of truths satisfies the basic condition of not containing pairs of the form:

The F is G and The F is not G.

This is because G either appears above F in the (unique correct) tree showing F, or it does not. Or to put it the other way: G either appears or does not appear in the account of what it is to be an F.[5]

We can easily appreciate the advantages that clear realization that *pros heauto* truths are going to be the privileged class (instead of those about some population of superexemplifiers) had for Plato. First of all, the realization allows forms to have all the properties they ought to without any threat to the unqualified way in which the privileged truths must hold. The circumstance that

The Cat is identical (sc. with itself)

and

The Cat is not identical (sc. with The Dog)

does not threaten our understanding of what it is to be identical, or of what it is to be a cat. That is given by the *pros heauto* truths revealing the genus-species structures. In general, since we know that the truth conditions for an assertion *pros heauto* are distinct from those for an assertion *pros ta alla* that may be made by the same form of words, the holding of a "rolling-around" result *pros ta alla* will never imply rolling around in the class of the *pros heauto*.

The new way of picking out privileged truths has some welcome side results. For one thing, it removes one of the most counterintuitive consequences the epistemology of the *Republic* seemed to have: namely, that one could not make a transition from opinion to knowledge concerning the same object (since only forms were objects of knowledge, and only sensible particulars were objects of opinion). In the scheme of the *Parmenides,* one can start with possession of the less fundamental *(pros ta alla)* type of truth about a form and go on to obtain the more fundamental *(pros heauto)* type. Someone making that transition would be going from common awareness about the displays of and by the property in question to possession of the account of the property itself. To take an example, everyday beliefs that certain acts or people are just come under the *pros ta alla* truths about Justice; so do such observations as that Justice is different from Law-Abidingness. *Pros ta alla* truths like these can plausibly be claimed to be what one starts with. Moreover, someone who goes beyond this to realize that Justice is psychic harmony—its account according to Plato—would clearly have achieved an increase in understanding. But this has not involved any radical change in topic: the topic is always the same form.

In addition, the new scheme rescues sensible particulars from the extreme disfavor into which "Platonism" would have thrust them. For stress on the fact that they display properties in a confused and impure manner together with the supposition that other entities manage to display properties purely naturally gives rise to an impression that the way in which sensible particulars have their properties is importantly second-rate. However, the scheme of the *Parmenides* encourages no such attitude. It is true of all individuals, both forms and sensible particulars, that the truths about them *pros ta alla* include the rolling-around type. Thus sensible particulars *taken as exhibiters of properties* are not at all inferior to forms. But there is still a difference between the two, and it is in terms of this difference that the new scheme will express the ontological dependence of sensible particulars on forms. That is, the more basic status of forms manifests itself in the fact that only they, and not sensible particulars, figure in the fundamental truths, those *pros heauto*.

Throughout my study I have been careful to put things in terms of a contrast between the view Plato developed in the *Parmenides* and another kind of view that is rejected in that dialogue; I have avoided commitment on whether a view of this other kind was formerly Plato's own.[6] This is because I do not wish to enter the lists either of those who seek to show that at the time of writing the middle dialogues Plato was what I have been calling a " 'Platonist,' " or of their opponents, who would demonstrate that he was not. That said, it seems fitting to conclude my study with some consideration of what it has to contribute to the story of Plato's development.

Clearly, it adds to a tendency that has been growing in recent decades to abandon a story that was once standard. That story told of a rather unhappy career. Plato was meant to have started writing with a gracious compliment to his master,[7] the early or "Socratic" dialogues. The high literary achievement of the middle-period works was supposed to coincide with a philosophical high point: a heady and confident time of glorious dogmatism. This story then has it that, after a major crisis in which he himself attacked and actually destroyed the theory that was his masterpiece, Plato spent his last years in extensive critical activity. His now-failing literary powers produced the late dialogues as a record of this barren final period.

The *Parmenides* as a record of hopeless confusion figures crucially in this story of an unhappy career, representing as it is supposed to do Plato's sense of the unviability of Platonism, and so leaving no possible development the late dialogues could hope to achieve. Appreciation of our dialogue as making real progress on such basic points as to enable Plato clearly to answer the famous criticisms takes away the turning point crucial to the story. My interpretation of the *Parmenides* as developing rather than destroying Plato's program thus coheres very well with recent work on the late dialogues that has been finding positive and deep developments in them (usually by sustained attention to the arguments of an individual text). We are now in a position to tell a more satisfying kind of story. Instead of seeing the middle dialogues as a perfected edifice that the late works then tear down, we can think of the masterpieces of the middle period as showing the need for work that the difficult final dialogues in fact take on.

A version of the new story that appeals to me is as follows. In the early dialogues Plato showed, following Socrates, that people who might have been expected to have knowledge on various matters turned out not to. They were revealed in this condition in a series of elenctic confrontations, by being unable to sustain discussion on the subjects of their supposed expertise without falling into contradiction. The middle works then presented Plato's own theories of these matters, including justice, love, the soul, and rhetoric. These theories rested on a metaphysical sketch, and in effect Plato claimed that the failures of others resulted from their ignorance of metaphysics.

But the extreme brevity of the passages devoted to metaphysics in the middle dialogues indicates that laying down dogmatically the tenets of a mature theory is not their main task. Thus I regard these passages as indicating the motivations and outlines of views that it is not their purpose fully to develop. Indeed, I believe these passages underdetermine the "theory" to be attributed to their author. It can come as a surprise on rereading these passages to see how much more specific are the doctrines on sensible particulars to which Plato commits himself than are those on forms. We have here one of the most effective uses of Plato's *chiaroscuro*[8] technique: he makes the main point he needs in context while leaving many difficult issues about forms in the shadows. Thus the language of the middle dialogues has some tendency to suggest—but is not sufficient to demonstrate—that Plato was a "Platonist." And so, as soon as we follow his advice to start taking forms seriously, we find ourselves asking such questions as whether they are superexemplifiers, what participation is, and so on.

I believe that Plato composed the first part of the *Parmenides* in order to bring his middle-period description of forms into the spotlight, and so to exhibit where it was lacking. The dialogue as a whole shows that he himself had turned his attention to the development of the views that were formerly sketched, treating them at a new level of sophistication and detail. The work of the *Parmenides* does not complete any theory, but it achieves major success in setting one up. We can look to the other late dialogues for the further development of Plato's program.

NOTES

Chapter 1

1. By "the second part of the dialogue" I mean from 137c4 to the end. (My citations follow the line numbering of Burnet's Oxford Classical Text, despite the improvements carried out in the Budé edition of Diès, since Burnet's seems to me to be the edition most widely available. When matters of editing are relevant to our inquiry, I will be providing pertinent information.)

2. Surveys of the secondary literature on the *Parmenides* can be found in the following studies: F. M. Cornford, *Plato and Parmenides;* R. E. Allen, *Plato's Parmenides;* and Mitchell Miller, Jr., *Plato's Parmenides.*

3. *Tht.* 183e5–184a1; *Soph.* 217c4–7.

4. While authors I group together here as following a single pattern all agree that the arguments they discuss are, so to speak, trying to follow the *reductio*-strategy, there is important disagreement among them on the question whether Plato knew what the trouble was, or whether he remained unable to see this and even unable to formulate his argument correctly. But I group them together because Gregory Vlastos (the leading exponent of the latter opinion) takes for granted that *we* should approach (an argument from) the passage by making an explicit and formal reconstruction of the argument, and by diagnosing the trouble. The papers of Vlastos on this subject are cited in n. 15.

5. Other writers (including K. Sayre, from whose treatment in *Plato's Late Ontology* I have learned the most, as well as R. E. Allen and M. Miller, whose works are cited in n. 2), have already begun to argue against this approach. But the prestige of the authors who followed the pattern just described, and the inclusion of their papers in influential and widely available collections, make the pattern one that is still dominant. Partly for this reason, and partly because my detailed views are different from those of other authors, I will go on to offer my own discussion.

6. I do not mean to suggest that those who have worked on the first part of the dialogue in isolation would explicitly endorse the claim that it can be fully understood without reference to the second part of the dialogue. They may well have been proceeding on the sensible plan of starting by getting clear on what was most manageable. But this still leaves their work open to the charge that their approach is inappropriate. Moreover, whether or not the authors of these papers believed that approaching these arguments in isolation was the ideal way to handle Plato's text, their articles have had the effect of leading

many readers to suppose that it is—since it is the procedure of so much influential work.

7. The idea that Plato meant the exercise to help just by providing an occasion to develop one's ability to deal with fallacious arguments is implausible: why should he bother to produce a text of some thirty pages when a vast body of fallacious arguments was already in existence? He must then have thought that something about these particular arguments was specially relevant to the famous difficulties.

8. T. Irwin's discussion in *Plato's Moral Theory* has played a major role in the controversy. (But perhaps unfortunately for present purposes, it is scattered throughout the book.) An important recent pair of contributions is the exchange between G. Vlastos and R. Kraut in *Oxford Studies in Ancient Philosophy*, vol. 1.

9. The phrase occurs on page 254 in "The Third Man Argument in the 'Parmenides,' " as reprinted in *Studies in Plato's Metaphysics*.

10. I do not wish to take a stand on what Plato's private views were during the middle period; I attribute insufficient development only to the views *as they appear* in the dialogues of that time. I do not know how to decide between the positions (i) that Plato's own views were no more developed, and (ii) that Plato had adequate views whose exposition he considered out of place given the subject matter and purpose of the works in question.

11. Here and in what follows, I do not mean by calling a certain view about what participation is "Anaxagorean" that Anaxagoras was the only person to hold the view, or even that he originated it. I use his name merely because his use of the view is most familiar to us, and most accessible.

12. For discussions of Anaxagoras's physical theory in connection with Plato, see J. Brentlinger, "Incomplete Predicates and the Two-World Theory of the *Phaedo*," *Phronesis* (1972) and D. J. Furley, "Anaxagoras in Response to Parmenides," *Canadian Journal of Philosophy* (1976) Suppl.

13. This move will be familiar to readers of Plato's dialogues, so I will not explicate it.

14. See Alexander of Aphrodisias, *in Metaphysica* 84.21ff.

15. In Gregory Vlastos, "The Third Man Argument in the *Parmenides*," *Philosophical Review* (1954). Other notable contributions are those of W. Sellars, "Vlastos and 'The Third Man,' " *Philosophical Review* (1955); P. T. Geach, "The Third Man Again," *Philosophical Review* (1956); Colin Strang, "Plato and the Third Man," *Proceedings of the Aristotelian Society* (1963); and Vlastos again, "Plato's 'Third Man' Argument (*Parm.* 132A1–B2): Text and Logic," *Philosophical Quarterly* (1969), which has a useful bibliography of articles published on the subject between 1955 and 1972.

16. This makes the appropriateness of referring to Plato's argument as the "Third Man" questionable. But to depart from what has become an established practice this late in the day would create more confusion than it is

worth. In any case, any differences there may be between the cases of The Man and The Large will not be relevant to our discussion.

17. I take the content of this paragraph from a seminar of Michael Frede's at Princeton.

18. Kenneth Sayre suggests this in *Plato's Late Ontology*, pp. 34–36.

19. The second of these general results is not meant to follow from the first. Rather, they correspond to the two results I generated in the case of Arithmetic (that we do not know The Numbers, and that Arithmetic has no application to the sensible world). Plato states the first of the general results as a conclusion at 134b11–c2, the second at 134d11–e1.

20. My schematic discussion of kinds of interpretation is meant to help orient readers by locating my project. It cannot of course present the particular motivations and detailed views of specific authors, or serve as an adequate basis for the full assessment of their views.

21. To be extremely precise, we find almost no such expressions. In the last few lines of the first section of the dialectical exercise, the interlocutor does show increasing reluctance to accept the conclusions presented to him. But these lines are an unusual case, and the conclusions in question seem to be included in general summaries the interlocutor accepts later (160b2–4 and 166c2–5). In any case rejecting these few results will of course not be enough for rejectionists, and the text contains no declaration of what makes these results unacceptable, which could guide us in going on to reject results from other sections.

22. One brand of rejectionism, that of Ryle (in "Plato's *Parmenides*," *Mind* [1939]) is immune to difficulties three and four. On this view, it is the hypotheses themselves that are unacceptable, and their leading to systematically contradictory results is what shows it. But Rylean rejectionism suffers from enough of the other difficulties to be implausible, and as far as I know has no longer any adherents.

23. In his important paper on the *Parmenides*, unfortunately rather misleadingly named "Notes on Ryle's Plato," in *Ryle*, ed. O. P. Wood and G. Pitcher.

24. The most tempting reading is that "Plato realised . . . that antinomies necessarily arise from the attempt to make any concept whatsoever . . . a subject of attributes" ("Plato's 'Parmenides,' " p. 117 as reprinted in *Studies in Plato's Metaphysics*, ed. R. E. Allen). Ryle himself resisted this particular temptation.

25. I. M. Crombie in *An Examination of Plato's Doctrines*, vol. 2, p. 339. Similar positions are those of J. M. Moravscik (in terms of "metaphysical atoms", in "Forms and Dialectic in the Second Half of the *Parmenides*," in *Language and Logos*, ed. M. Schofield and M. Nussbaum) and P. K. Curd (in terms of forms as absolute unities which can each be called by only one name, in "Some Problems of Unity in the First Hypothesis of the *Parmenides*," *Southern Journal of Philosophy* (1989)).

26. "I suggest that the One stands in for all the Forms," in "Some Problems," p. 348.

27. For example, those of Cornford, *Plato and Parmenides,* and of Sayre, *Plato's Late Ontology.*

28. This will emerge from our study of Parmenides' methodological remarks, in chapter 2. It is also implied by the talk of returning once again to the hypothesis (142b1–2) and, in the case of the negative hypothesis, by the talk of going once again back to the start (165e2).

Chapter 2

1. Indeed, Cornford did follow Wundt. But since there has been no change in the editions people use, by now Wundt's conjecture is virtually forgotten.

2. The machinery creaks here as in the actual exercise, because of tension between faithful characterization of what the Eleatics were doing and fictive presentation of treatment of The Many and The One as research into forms.

3. B. Jowett, trans., *The Dialogues of Plato,* 3rd ed., vol. 4, p. 57.

4. This point is unaffected by the circumstance that one's original hypothesis *itself* may have been of the form "A is not." Then its negation would be "A is," and this negation of the original hypothesis is what Reading 1a fails to prescribe.

5. I will not bore readers further with a discussion of all the other readings compatible with this change in punctuation. The discussion of the first group of interpretations will have made it possible for anyone who might be interested to see why I prefer the reading I do.

6. I am grateful to David Furley for pointing out to me that, given 135e5–6, *hotioun allo pathos paschontos* here covers, for example, being unlike just as well as being like.

7. The exact order of the sections I have listed here as V through VIII is underdetermined by the text, which specifies deriving results "for The One and The Many in relation to themselves and in relation to each other."

8. There is in fact some controversy over the number of sections of argument that should be recognized. The two possibilities are eight or nine. I will be proceeding temporarily on the assumption that there are indeed eight. I will make clear (in chapter 6, when we come to its place in the exercise) what status I assign to the passage (155e4–157b5) that some take as an extra section.

9. Thus we should translate 136b6–c5 as follows. "And in a word, concerning whatever you hypothesize as being or as not being or as suffering any other affection, you must examine the consequences in relation to itself and in relation to each one of the others, whichever you pick out, and in relation to more and in relation to all in the same way, and ⟨you must examine the

consequences for⟩ the others in turn in relation to themselves and in relation to another whichever you choose, ⟨all of this⟩ if what you hypothesized is the case, and also if it is not, if you are going to discern the truth accurately, having exercised completely." (I take it that the spelling out at 136c1–2: *pros hen hekaston tōn allōn . . . kai pros pleiō kai pros sumpanta hōsautōs* simply results from being specific about what falls under: in relation to the others.)

10. Because of the location of the dialectic within the program of Platonist metaphysics, and Parmenides' statement that one should take as subjects things "which are specially apprehended by discourse and can be regarded as Forms" (135e2–4, translated by Cornford), it is right to take "The One" to be a Platonic form rather than the single being investigated by the historical Parmenides.

11. R. E. Allen, *Plato's Parmenides*, p. 15 and pp. 182–83; Richard Robinson, *Plato's Earlier Dialectic*, pp. 245–46.

12. I suppose it could be claimed to mean: . . . if it is not The One . . . But since I am not aware of anyone's supporting this reading, and since it does not fit the arguments of the section at all, I will not complicate matters by discussing this possibility further.

13. All the ambiguous formulations are at least compatible with this.

14. It is of course extremely common for Greek sentences to leave "is" to be understood, and both candidate translations of this phrase supply it.

15. *Platons Parmenides*, fn. 1, p. 6; Cornford, *Plato and Parmenides*, p. 108.

16. There is still the minor infelicity that Parmenides says he is starting from *his* hypothesis of The One. But we need not remove this: it is part of the creaking of the machinery that is inevitable given (what cannot be doubted) that Plato presents a character who has some of the traits of the historical Eleatic but is also a researcher into Platonic forms.

Chapter 3

1. K. Sayre deserves credit for drawing attention to the fact that the qualifications have an important role in generating sections of argument (first in "Plato's *Parmenides*: Why the Eight Hypotheses are Not Contradictory," *Phronesis* (1978) and then in *Plato's Late Ontology*. What he does not do successfully, in my opinion, is develop an understanding of the *force* of the qualifications. Thus he produces a combination of multisubjectism and rejectionism.

2. There is in fact a great contrast between the language of the methodological advice and the summaries of the results of the dialectic on the one hand, and that of the actual arguments on the other. While the in-relation-to qualifications occur very prominently in the former, Plato uses them extremely

sparingly in the latter. I can only suppose this to be part of his program of making us work actively, with written work providing at most an occasion for thought.

3. As noted earlier, there is some controversy over whether we should recognize eight or nine sections. I will be proceeding on the assumption that there are indeed only eight coordinate sections, and will show when I come to its place in the text what status I accord to the passage some take as an additional section.

4. There is a textual problem here. When we come to this passage, I will be arguing in favor of adopting Heindorf's conjecture. For the moment I have simply adopted it. But the occurrence of the *pros* phrases is not in doubt, in any case.

5. See for example H. W. Smyth, *Greek Grammar* and Liddell, Scott, and Jones (LSJ).

6. I specify and discuss the "canonical list of predicates" in chapter 6.

7. I will turn to such application in chapters 9 and 10.

8. 102a10–103a2. This language of the *Phaedo* is echoed in the first part of the *Parmenides* (130b3 ff.).

9. The idea is that Plato and Aristotle will consider as *ousia* whatever turns out to have a certain functional role. This is why Aristotle considers himself, Plato, and various Presocratics as all making rival identifications of *ousia*. (I take this point from Michael Frede's graduate seminar on *Metaphysics* Z at Princeton.)

10. These will turn out not to be the only cases; but they are the central ones, and the other cases will be in a certain way derivative from these. I will treat this issue at the beginning of chapter 5.

11. I in fact believe that no individual is identical with any nature; but this will depend on the development of some complicated views that will not occur until later.

12. *Plato and Parmenides*, pp. 123–24.

13. Cornford himself will ultimately reject this subject.

14. I base this example on the discussion in Gosling's commentary, *Plato "Philebus,"* p. 156 ff.). Obviously it sketches the tree in question only partially.

15. The kinds of the late dialogues are forms. The play in the use of *eidos* that allows it to be used for both makes this identification natural in Greek in a way that is less evident in English translation.

16. My use of "A is B" never carried commitment to the necessary appearance of the word "is."

17. Indeed, assuming (as is generally done) that Plato believed division not to proceed so far as to yield Callias, nothing can be correctly predicated *pros heauto* of Callias.

18. On the *Sophist*, see Michael Frede's *Prädikation und Existenzaussage*.

19. It also resolves a puzzlement I used to feel about the *Sophist:* why Plato relied on the distinction between the *kath' hauto* and *pros allo* uses of "is" not only without explaining it, but without even drawing our attention to its importance. It now seems to me that he felt he could do this because of the fanfare he gave the distinction when he introduced it in the *Parmenides.*

Chapter 4

1. "Good" in this context means valid, sound, from an unambiguous hypothesis, and instructive.

2. Here and in what follows, I will use Cornford's view as representative of the multiple-subject interpretation, even though his ultimate rejection of the subject of this first section of arguments makes his interpretation of the mixed type and prevents it from being typical of multiple-subject efforts. I have chosen his comments for discussion because his book is widely available and still widely consulted, because he states very clearly what his views are, and, most important, because the entirety of his commentary is extant.

3. *Plato and Parmenides,* pp. 116–17

4. *Plato and Parmenides,* p. 114

5. Cornford here seems to have imported the weaknesses in his interpretation of the historical Parmenides into his interpretation of Plato's work.

6. By this point decision over what to capitalize and what not has become difficult. But it also doesn't matter much, since the contrast in question corresponds to nothing in Plato's Greek.

7. *Plato and Parmenides,* pp. 120–21.

8. Actually these considerations leave a gap in proving that The One is not in motion *pros heauto:* The One could still be in motion *pros heauto* in virtue of the identity of the two natures Unity and Motion. But their nonidentity is so obvious that the gap does not seem particularly dangerous.

9. At this point something odd about the strategy of the passage as I explicated it emerges. If we are going from the outset on the assumption that The One will only be the same *pros heauto* if the natures in question are identical—that is, that it is implausible to consider One a species of Same—then we are going on an assumption that already includes rejection of the claim that The One is the same as itself *pros heauto.* It seems to me that the following considerations bear on this. (i) The defeat of the identity between the natures of The One and The Same is the interesting result really, and it allows Plato to demonstrate an important procedure (the counterexample method of defeating proposed identities). But (ii) casting the passage so that the final result is "The One is not the same as itself" (a) makes a better complement to the preceding result that it is not other than another, and (b) is more paradoxical at first blush. Thus the arrangement of the passage as a whole is suited

to the complex purpose of the dialectical display. Its initial air of paradox challenges us to work to find out what is going on; and once we understand the project, its central portion displays an important procedure to yield a non-trivial result.

10. This thought may seem anachronistic in connection with Plato. But 129c4–d2 indicates that he did associate speaking of something as one with completion specifying one what.

11. Cf. Jowett, *Dialogues of Plato:* . . . likeness is sameness of affections.

12. It is important not to be carelessly misled by the occurrence of the word *peponthe* into thinking we are talking about features of The One and not its nature. *Peponthe* here as I take it rather has the function of saying: if this *happened to* The One . . .

13. But not because every Aristotelian individual has at most one Aristotelian essence! It is, rather, because our scheme associates one nature with each form.

14. I am not sure whether this applies to the final lines of the section, roughly 141e ff., but the increasing uncertainty and rejection of conclusions by the interlocutor set these lines apart from the rest in any case.

Chapter 5

1. Commentators are not agreed on the question whether this One is the same as the subject of the first section of arguments, or a new subject. But this does not affect the broad agreement on the *kind* of results we have here: results about what features the section's subject has.

2. See for example Burnet ap. Cornford, *Plato and Parmenides,* p. 153 n. 1, and J. M. Moravcsik, "Forms and Dialectic in the Second Half of the *Parmenides,"* esp. p. 143.

3. I do not mean that they do not reject middle-period Platonism as a philosophical position, but only that they do not use "rejectionism" as the basis of their interpretation of Plato's middle dialogues.

4. Or, perhaps, the passages pointed out that *accounts* of qualities like Beauty and Justice in terms of sensible qualities applied also to cases that are in fact ugly and unjust.

5. I now find that my view of this passage is in substantial agreement with that of P. Curd in *"Parmenides* 142b5–144e7: The 'Unity is Many' Arguments," *Southern Journal of Philosophy* (1990). I retain my own discussion because of the instructive way it connects with my larger interpretation.

6. Of course, (6) is not grounded by facts only about the display of Justice; its grounding must include facts in which entities unnamed in (6) display Health.

7. This statement only applies to the kinds of facts (those involving displaying) that back assertions *pros ta alla.*

8. *Plato's Late Ontology,* pp. 54ff.

9. I take *to elachiston* adverbially with Jowett, Cornford, Diès, and Curd.

10. In translating this and the preceding demonstration, I follow Cornford in sometimes using "Unity" to translate *to hen* when it produces more natural English than rigid adherence to the translation "The One."

11. In fact one might question whether there is such a thing as M-ness here; but even if there is, the parts a, b, c . . . do not display it.

12. Plato is generally agreed to take this principle as covering opposites in a broad sense that includes what I have been calling contradictories as well as what I have been calling opposites. The principle is stated and illustrated with examples at 436b8–437a2.

13. Presumably another treatment along the lines of our present one—discussing relevant qualifications—would explain how "The One is older than the others" and "The One is younger than the others" can both have been established.

14. Another source of qualifications relevant to the test could be the identity of the others (see previous note). But since our present passage draws no attention to this, I will not discuss it further.

15. The translation is that of Jowett, *Dialogues of Plato,* except that I have capitalized "The One" to preserve consistency with my exposition.

Chapter 6

1. At least, this is the mainstream Neoplatonist view.

2. So Cornford writes (*Plato and Parmenides,* p. 194) that 155e4–157b5 "has no claim to the status, which many assign to it, of a ninth independent Hypothesis. That would destroy the symmetry of the whole set of Hypotheses."

3. For convenience, I have numbered only the eight sections that are definitely coordinate sections.

4. This was not discussed as a separate topic in the first hypothesis, but the issue of touching figures in 138a2 ff.

5. *"Tithenai ta phainomena,"* in *Aristote et les problèmes de methode,* ed. S. Mansion, p. 97; discussion of the group then continues for pages.

6. Miller, *Plato's Parmenides,* p. 116. Cornford makes a similar suggestion in *Plato and Parmenides,* p. 195.

7. This appears on pp. 4–5, T. Irwin, "Plato's Heracleiteanism," *Philosophical Quarterly* (1977).

Chapter 7

1. At this point there is a switch in singular and plural forms induced by the fact that we have moved on to get results for the others. Since the others are plural while The One (i.e. what is other than the others) is singular, we now have "in relation to themselves," and "in relation to the other."

2. Cornford *Plato and Parmenides,* pp. 204–13; Sayre, *Plato's Late Ontology,* pp. 63–67; Allen, *Plato's Parmenides,* pp. 268–73. As usual there is variation on many points, including the identity of The One and the others. Nevertheless, the basic understanding of the way the section proceeds seems to me substantially the same.

3. Allen (*Plato's Parmenides*) considers the linguistic similarity to the *Philebus* superficial only; the others believe it reflects doctrinal continuity. Sayre (*Plato's Late Ontology*) takes up the *Philebus* and continues his discussion of Aristotle's reports in his central chaps. 2 and 3; the others make all their remarks in their discussions of our text, cited in the preceding note.

4. This step is, I think, the only part of the argument about which there is some variation in scholarly opinion. I prefer the version I give here, because it avoids fallacy.

5. "Ordinary" uses of *eidos* are frequent. To take only a scattering of those appearing in the *Republic:* 439e2, 475b5, 510d5, 559e6, 572a6, 590c4, 618a8. But the *Republic* also uses *eidos* to stand specially for Platonic forms, e.g., at 476a5, 510b8, 511c1, 511c2, 596a6, 597a2, 597c8. Notice that some passages—notably the comparison of philosophers and lovers of spectacle, and the Divided Line—contain both uses.

6. Plato uses *kath' heauto* in this way, to isolate one member of a collection, in the *Parmenides* at 158a1–3.

Chapter 8

1. The narrower use of "principle" to refer only to propositions is of course a special case of the wider use basic in antiquity.

2. 161a6–b4 and 161c7–d1

3. At least it works for those who would grant the requisite claims in the philosophy of language.

Chapter 9

1. At least the feat seems impossible in many cases. For Largeness it will be problematic. But examples can be multiplied. To take another, this "the-

ory" seems committed to taking Manyness as the single (!) most multitudinous thing.

Chapter 10

1. W. G. Runciman makes a similar point on p. 154 of "Plato's *Parmenides*," reprinted in *Studies in Plato's Metaphyics*, ed. R. E. Allen.

2. I am grateful to Sally Haslanger, John Cooper, and David Furley for pointing this out to me.

3. Because examples are so numerous, I choose four at random. The language of participation occurs in connection with *pros heauto* cases at 137e1 and 140c5; in connection with those *pros ta alla* at 144a7–9 and 158b6–9.

4. Those to whom it is not yet familiar might start with the final six Stephanus pages of *Republic* V, together with the stretch of text devoted to The Sun, The Line, and The Cave, that is from roughly 506d to 518b.

5. The occurrences of "or" in this and the preceding sentence are meant to be read in the exclusive sense.

6. I have committed myself to an uncontroversial observation on the characteristic pattern of Plato's assertions in the middle dialogues, but have tried to avoid commitment on whether or not he subscribed to the totality of the view I have been calling " 'Platonism.' "

7. I owe this phrase to Richard McKim.

8. I borrow this charming phrase from Vlastos, p. 107 in "Reasons and Causes in the *Phaedo*," as reprinted in *Platonic Studies*.

BIBLIOGRAPHY

Allen, R. E. *Plato's Parmenides*. Minneapolis: University of Minnesota Press, 1983.

Bostock, D. *Plato's "Phaedo."* Oxford: Clarendon Press, 1986.

Brentlinger, J. "Incomplete Predicates and the Two-World Theory of the *Phaedo*." *Phronesis* 17 (1972), 61–79.

Burnet, J., ed. *Platonis Opera*. Vol. 2. Oxford: Clarendon Press, 1901.

Cornford, F. M. *Plato and Parmenides*. London: Routledge and Kegan Paul, 1939.

Crombie, I. M. *An Examination of Plato's Doctrines*. Vol. 2. London: Routledge and Kegan Paul, 1963.

Curd, P. K. "*Parmenides* 142b5–144e7: The 'Unity is Many' Arguments." *Southern Journal of Philosophy* 28, no. 1 (1990), 19–35.

———. "Some Problems of Unity in the First Hypothesis of the *Parmenides*." *Southern Journal of Philosophy* 27, no. 3 (1989), 347–59.

Diès, A., ed. *Platon: Oeuvres complètes*. Vol. 8 Paris: Société d'Édition "Les Belles Lettres," 1923.

Frede, Michael. *Prädikation und Existenzaussage. Hypomnemata*, no. 18. Göttingen: Vandenhoeck & Ruprecht, 1967.

Furley, D. J. "Anaxagoras in Response to Parmenides." In *New Essays on Plato and the Pre-Socratics*, ed. R. A. Shiner and J. King-Farlow. *Canadian Journal of Philosophy* Suppl. 2 (1976), 61–85.

Geach, P. T. "The Third Man Again." *Philosophical Review* 65 (1956), 72–82.

Gosling, J. C. B. *Plato "Philebus."* Oxford: Clarendon Press, 1975.

Heinforf, F., ed. *Platonis Dialogi Selecti*. Vol. 3. Berlin, 1806.

Irwin, T. "Plato's Heracleiteanism." *Philosophical Quarterly* 27, no. 106 (1977), 1–13.

———. *Plato's Moral Theory*. Oxford: Clarendon Press, 1977.

Jowett, B., trans. *The Dialogues of Plato*. Vol. 4. 3rd ed. Oxford: Clarendon Press, 1892.

Kraut, R. "Comments on Gregory Vlastos, 'The Socratic Elenchus.' " In *Oxford Studies in Ancient Philosophy*, vol. 1, ed. Julia Annas. Oxford: Clarendon Press, 1983, pp. 59–70.

Liddell, H. G., and R. Scott. *A Greek-English Lexicon*. 9th ed. Rev. H. S. Jones and R. McKenzie. Oxford: Clarendon Press, 1940; with supplement, 1968.

186   Bibliography

Manutius, Aldus, ed. *Omnia Platonis Opera.* Venice, 1513.

Miller, Mitchell, Jr. *Plato's Parmenides.* Princeton, N.J.: Princeton University Press, 1986.

Moravscik, J. M. "Forms and Dialectic in the Second Half of the *Parmenides.*" In *Language and Logos,* ed. M. Schofield and M. Nussbaum. Cambridge: Cambridge University Press, 1982, pp. 135–53.

Owen, G. E. L. "Aristotle on Time." In *Motion and Time, Space and Matter: Interrelations in the History of Philosophy and Science,* ed. P. Machamer and R. Turnbull. Columbus: Ohio State University Press, 1976, pp. 3–27.

———. "Notes on Ryle's Plato." In *Ryle,* ed. O. P. Wood and G. Pitcher. Garden City, N.Y.: Doubleday, 1970, pp. 341–72.

———. "*Tithenai ta phainomena.*" In *Aristote et les problèmes de méthode,* ed. S. Mansion. Louvain: Publications Universitaires de Louvain, 1961, pp. 83–103.

Proclus. *Commentarium in Platonis Parmenidem.* Ed. V. Cousin. Paris, 1864.

Robinson, R. *Plato's Earlier Dialectic.* 2nd ed. Oxford: Clarendon Press, 1953.

Runciman, W. G. "Plato's *Parmenides.*" *Harvard Studies in Classical Philology* 64 (1959), 89–120. Rpt. in *Studies in Plato's Metaphysics,* ed. R. E. Allen. London: Routledge and Kegan Paul, 1965, pp. 149–84.

Ryle, G. "Plato's *Parmenides.*" *Mind* 48 (1939), 129–51, 302–25. Rpt. in *Studies in Plato's Metaphysics,* ed. R. E. Allen. London: Routledge and Kegan Paul, 1965, pp. 97–147.

Sayre, K. M. *Plato's Late Ontology.* Princeton, N.J.: Princeton University Press, 1983.

———. "Plato's *Parmenides:* Why the Eight Hypotheses are Not Contradictory." *Phronesis* Vol. 23, No. 2 (1978) pp. 133–50.

Sellars, W. "Vlastos and the Third Man." *Philosophical Review* 64, no. 3 (1955) 405–37.

Smith, C. F. trans. *Thucydides: History of the Peloponnesian War.* Loeb Classical Library. Cambridge: Mass.: Harvard University Press, 1919.

Smyth, H. W. *Greek Grammar.* 1920. Rpt. Cambridge, Mass.: Harvard University Press, 1956.

Stephanus [Henri Estienne], ed. *Platonis opera quae extant omnia.* Paris: 1578.

Strang, C. "Plato and the Third Man." *Proceedings of the Aristotelian Society* Suppl. 37 (1963), 147–64. Rpt. in *Plato I,* ed. G. Vlastos. Garden City, N.Y.: Doubleday, 1971, pp. 184–200.

Thucydides. *De Bello Peloponnesiaco.* Trans. Thomas Hobbes. 2nd ed. London, 1676.

Vlastos, G. "The Socratic Elenchus." In *Oxford Studies in Ancient Philosophy,* vol. 1, ed. Julia Annas. Oxford: Clarendon Press, 1983, pp. 27–58; with "Afterthoughts on the Socratic Elenchus," pp. 71–74.

————. "Plato's 'Third Man' Argument (*Parm*. 132A1–B2): Text and Logic."
Philosophical Quarterly 19, no. 77 (1969), 289–301.

————. "Reasons and Causes in the *Phaedo*." *Philosophical Review* 78, no.
3 (1969), 291–325. Rpt. in *Platonic Studies*. Princeton, N.J.: Princeton
University Press, 1973; with corrections, 1981, pp. 76–110.

————. "The Third Man Argument in the *Parmenides*." *Philosophical Review* 63, no. 3 (1954), 319–49. Rpt. in *Studies in Plato's Metaphysics*,
ed. R. E. Allen. London: Routledge and Kegan Paul, 1965, pp. 231–63.

Wundt, M. *Platons Parmenides*. Stuttgart and Berlin: Verlag W. Kohlhammer, 1935.

INDEX

Abstraction, project of, 135–39
Aldine edition, 35–36
Allen, R. E., 40, 132, 173 *n.* 2, 173 *n.*
  5, 177 *n.* 11, 182 *n.* 2
Analytic/synthetic distinction, 72
Anaxagorean conception of participation,
  11, 14–15, 157, 159
Aristotle
  Physics influenced by *Parmenides*,
    123–24
  Plato's metaphysics as reported by,
    133
  Politics extract, 52
  Rhetoric extract, 51
  Third Man Argument popularized by,
    15
Aristotle (the interlocutor), 21–22

Brentlinger, J., 174 *n.* 12
Burnet, J., 29, 31–32, 35, 38, 143, 173
  n. 1, 180 *n.* 2

Cats, three smallest become three best-
  fed, 90
Change
  distinction between *a*- and *s*-, 128–29
  moment of, 126–29
Chiaroscuro technique, Plato's, 171
Collection and division, 67–70. *See also*
  Genus-species trees
Consequent of schema, qualifications
  added to, 65
Contradictions
  dialectic's results seem systematically
    to produce, 19
  do not, after all, obtain between results
    of first two sections, 77–79
  seen by second main type of

interpretation as merely apparent,
  23–26
Cooper, John, 183 *n.* 2
Cornford, F. M., 24–25, 44, 64–65, 78,
  80–81, 84–85, 127, 132, 143, 173
  n. 2, 176 *n.* 1, 176 *n.* 27, 177 *n.*
  15, 178 *n.* 13, 179 *n.* 2, 182 *n.* 2
Creaking of machinery (in portraying
  Eleatics), 176 *n.* 2, 177 *n.* 16
Crombie, I. M., 175 *n.* 25
Curd, P. K., 23, 175 *n.* 25, 176 *n.* 26,
  180 *n.* 5

Day model, 14
Demosthenes, 52
Development, Plato's, 170–72. *See also*
  Forms; Participation; Privileged
  truths, Plato's interest in marking
  off; Socrates
  Parmenides as representing crucial
    moment in, 3, 162–63
Dialectical exercise, 19
  actual departures from general ordering
    of, 133, 145–47
  eight essential number of sections of,
    117–24
  minor variation in descriptions'
    ordering of, 132
  overall grouping within, 132
  structure of, 30–38
  unexplained qualifications cause
    opacity in description of, 20, 45, 46
Diès, A., 29, 32, 35, 38, 143, 173 *n.* 1

Eidos, Plato's use of, 135, 178 *n.* 15,
  182 *n.* 5
Essential/accidental distinction, 72
Euthyphro, genus-species trees in, 69–70

189